A Bonefishing Journey

To Charles
Best wishes
Graham Stephen

A Bonefishing Journey

Graham Stephens

Loddon Press

First published in hardback in Great Britain in 2011 by Loddon Press.

Copyright © Graham Stephens 2011

The moral right of Graham Stephens to be identified as the author of this work has been asserted by him in accordance of the Copyright, Design and Patent Act of 1988.

All rights reserved. No part of this publication may be reproduced, stored in a retrieval system, or transmitted in any form or by any means, electronic, mechanical, photocopying, recording or otherwise, without the prior permission of both the copyright owner and the above publisher of this book.

A CIP catalogue record for this book is available from the British Library.

Hardback ISBN: 978-0-9570523-0-7

Design by Alan Gooch

Printed and bound in the UK by the MPG Books Group,
Bodmin and King's Lynn

Loddon Press
25 St Michaels Close
North Waltham
Hampshire
RG25 2BP

www.bonefishingjourney.com

Papers used by Loddon Press contain wood from well-managed forests, certified in accordance with the strict environmental, social and economic standards of the Forest Stewardship Council.

To Sue, Stuart and Duncan

Contents

Introduction		11
Chapter 1.	Anegada	18
Chapter 2.	Eleuthera	29
Chapter 3.	Los Roques	39
Chapter 4.	Long Island	52
Chapter 5.	Virgin Gorda	63
Chapter 6.	Andros	69
Chapter 7.	Harbour Island	84
Chapter 8.	Joulter Cays	94
Chapter 9.	Cayo Largo	108
Chapter 10.	Cayo Coco	118
Chapter 11.	Punta Allen	131
Chapter 12.	Bonefish Stuff	145
Chapter 13.	Getting There	157
Chapter 14.	Tactics	166
Chapter 15.	Gotcha	178
Chapter 16.	Other Flies	186
Chapter 17.	Boats	193
Acknowledgements		202

Introduction

It's late in the afternoon, the sun is becoming increasingly low in the sky and the light is changing. I'm standing on a flat of dense turtle grass and the ankle-deep water, despite being crystal clear, appears dark green. Way off in the distance I first hear and then see some disturbance in the shallow water, as a pod of big bonefish erupt and I watch the fish bolt in different directions. They are tailing bonefish and very spooky, but I haven't caused their panic and nor has Trevor, or Phillip our guide, who are two distant specks far away, as is our skiff which is anchored up a long way from us all.

This is the moment I have been waiting and hoping for all day. The tide has been steadily falling for the past few hours and the tight schools of agitated bonefish have now dispersed across the flat. They are making the most of what will be for them, just an hour or two when they can feed, unmolested by sharks and barracuda, in the secure comfort of the warm, shallow water. But of course, despite the relative safety of the shallow turtle grass flat, the bonefish have not managed to shed millions of years of conditioned neurosis. They will continue to erupt and bolt from their shadows until the water becomes so shallow that, as if by magic, they will be gone and the flat will be just an empty patchwork of exposed sand and puddles and the scene I am witnessing and part of, will be a memory.

But for now they are still there and I have the opportunity to indulge in the very pinnacle of bonefishing and catch some tailing bonefish. As I scan the water I can see bonefish tails everywhere, but I need to have a plan and not simply target the first tailing fish that comes into view. I can see some fish maybe 50 yards away, moving to my right and there are the tails of three or perhaps four good-sized bonefish slowly gliding around hoping for a juicy crab or shrimp to pounce on. But I know that there will probably be other bonefish between them and where I am standing that have not yet shown themselves and I don't want to spook them – all I need to see is a tail that will betray their presence.

I stand and wait and scan the water and then suddenly, to my left, a big, glistening tail emerges slowly from the water and then I can see the dorsal fin too. The fish stops for a moment, then quivers before suddenly lunging head first into weed and I can clearly see the whole tail end of a big bonefish and it's the one I will fish for. The bonefish is much closer than the others, but I still need to make up ground so that I can be in the correct position to get in one good cast. I walk, oh so slowly, never taking my eyes

Introduction

off the fish, or where I think the fish is, and watch as the tail occasionally disappears before re-emerging another yard or so further ahead, and I know that in just a few more steps I will be in the right spot to cast.

My fly is a Borski Shrimp with no eyes, so that it doesn't make too much sound as it enters the water, and an essential weed guard to stop it fouling on the turtle grass. If I can get the fly within a couple of feet of the fish and just wait until it is close enough to see it, I only need to twitch the fly and the bonefish will nail it. But that's a lot of ifs!

The bonefish is now about 10 yards away and I am crouching down casting. The fly does land 2 feet away but the fish changes direction just as the fly is about to hit the surface of the water and it is now moving away from the fly instead of towards it, so I will have to recast. My heart is in my mouth as I gently, slowly, pull the fly back for another shot, but the fish is moving even further away and I have to follow it yet again. It then turns to the right and I get off another cast and the fly lands 4 feet away from the bonefish which is a little further than I would wish, but if the bonefish doesn't change direction then I am definitely in with a chance.

The fish suddenly stops with its dorsal fin and tail fin showing above the water and I wonder if it has sensed something, but I think not. I am crouching down and hardly breathing. So far I haven't made a wrong move so I just hold my breath a little longer and pray for the fish to start swimming again and continue on its path – and it does. The fish is now no more than a foot from the fly. Now is my chance and I move it slowly, just a few inches. The bonefish darts forward, the line twitches, I strip strike and the water erupts as the hooked fish heads for the horizon. This is what it is all about. This is why I go bonefishing and it doesn't come any better!

And now the fun starts. The fish is a good one and is charging across the flat in a blistering run, which is so fast that I can hear the fly line being ripped through the water. The end of the fly line went through the tip ring just a few seconds after I hooked the fish and there is now a long belly of backing connecting me to the bonefish which is now way off in the distance. I can clearly see the fish in the increasingly shallow water as it thrashes the surface with its glistening tail but, after two more equally lengthy runs, I manage to get some of the fly line back on the reel. The bonefish is doggedly circling me and for a short while it gives no ground, but eventually the fight starts to take an effect and when I finally get the chance I grab the leader then lift the bonefish gently from the water and gaze in wonder yet again, as I always do, at the beauty of the fish. The bonefish is a good one, at least 7 pounds and maybe even bigger, but the weight isn't the most important thing. What really matters is just being there and soaking up the whole bonefishing experience.

This scenario is not untypical and is one I have been fortunate to experience many times over the years. It is a perfect illustration of why bonefishing is so special. I

Introduction

often ask myself, if I could only fish for one species, with just one method, what would it be? The answer to what should be a difficult question for most anglers is, for me, very easy to answer. It is, not surprisingly, fly fishing for bonefish. So why is this?

A good starting point to answering this question and something in the bonefishes favour, is that they just happen to live and feed in some of the most beautiful places on Earth. Spending a day wading a flat should leave the angler wondering in awe at the unspoilt beauty and diversity of the habit before them. The sand flats, in their myriad of colours, which change with the tide and light throughout the fishing day, are magical places. The mangrove islands, home to so many different creatures and their accompanying cacophony of sounds, are equally precious and complex. Then there are the creeks that can go on for miles and which always give me a feeling of expectancy and excitement as the skiff weaves its way, often at speed, towards some unknown destination that rarely disappoints. Finally, there is the sky which, on a cloudless day, will merge with a flat so that there is no perceptible link at the horizon and everything appears blue and turquoise. This is a place where tourists rarely venture and which is the preserve of the bonefisher.

And then we get the opportunity to fly fish for bonefish; almost certainly the most graceful and elegant way to fish and one that allows the angler the opportunity to go, uncluttered, in search of their quarry. The bonefisher also gets the opportunity to see the take and there is no chuck and chance element involved. If the angler so wishes, every bonefish caught will have been spotted, cast to and then watched as they move towards and take the fly.

Once the fish is hooked, the angler gets the chance to play one of the fastest fish that you can catch and to watch a bonefish strip line from the reel until, on occasions, you wonder if you have enough backing, is always an exhilarating moment. The fight from a good-sized bonefish is legendary and rightly so. And then, once you grab the leader and gently lift the bonefish from the water you become aware, yet again, of the beauty of the fish; the brilliance of the scales, the elegant shape and that wonderful tail. In fact, a fish perfectly designed for the environment in which it has lived and survived for so long.

You would imagine that this is enough to warrant the bonefish its claim as a great fish to catch, but there is more. Bonefishing is not simply just fishing, it is also hunting, and to spend time, either on the front of a skiff or perhaps standing in warm, ankle-deep water watching and waiting for your quarry to suddenly appear is, for me, one of the great angling experiences. The air of expectation that accompanies this is almost as exhilarating as actually catching the fish itself.

This last point leads me nicely on to fishing for tailing bonefish and I can think of no other fish that gives the angler such an intimate fishing challenge. To stand on a bonefish flat and to see just a glint of a tail maybe

Introduction

100 yards away and then to move slowly in that direction, never taking your eyes off the spot where you first saw the fish, and then finally catching it, really is as good as it gets with a fishing rod. It also gives the angler the opportunity to fish on their own in a true wilderness environment.

There is of course, one final piece of the jigsaw that makes fishing for bonefish so special, and that is the people you meet along the way. Over the years I have had the privilege of meeting and finding new friends who have added greatly to the overall fishing experience. These have been anglers from many parts of the world and then of course, there are the guides who work so hard in the hot sun and who you can get to know very well over the course of a week's fishing.

Looking back at this list of what makes bonefishing so special for me there are, of course, many other fish that tick some of the boxes, but I don't know of any that tick all of them in the way the bonefish does. What I have tried to do in this book is to touch upon all of these facets of bonefishing and, hopefully, portray some of the great fishing experiences I have been fortunate enough to enjoy.

Chapter 1

Anegada

It all started in the mid 1970s. Sue had gone shopping and I was spending a lazy Saturday morning doing nothing in particular, but the television was on in the background and I noticed that there was a programme on about fishing. This was something of a rarity in those days and apart from Jack Hargreaves wonderful *Out of Town* series, there was very rarely anything about fishing on the box. What particularly grabbed my interest was that it concerned fly fishing and as a recent convert who had managed to catch a few small rainbow trout on the fly from Weir Wood Reservoir in Sussex, I stopped what little I was doing and sat down to watch.

What quickly became apparent to me was that the angler I was watching on the television was fly fishing, but that it bore no resemblance to my own experiences in Southern England. The scene was of three people in a boat, which I would come to realize much later was a skiff, and they were fly fishing in an area of sea that was incredibly shallow! It also looked very hot and sunny, so I guessed it was

Anegada

somewhere in the tropics. I was captivated by the concentration that all three of them put in to what they were doing; one was standing on a high platform at the back of the boat, scanning the water and obviously looking for something, whilst at the same time steering and propelling the boat with a very long pole. Only one angler appeared to be actually fishing and he was at the front of the boat, once again looking intently for something whilst holding his fly rod ready for action. The third member of the team, and they were clearly working together as one, was standing in the well of the boat and although obviously another angler, he wasn't fishing but looking for something just as the other two were.

I found this captivating and was intrigued to find out what they were fishing for, as I had missed the introduction to the programme that would, no doubt, have explained this. However, I was content to watch as the boat glided slowly and quietly between small mangrove islands and over the incredibly shallow water. This carried on for a while until quite suddenly all three crew members became agitated about something. The guy who was standing on the platform at the back of the boat had clearly seen or sensed something and started to give instructions to the angler at the front. Within seconds he was casting very fluidly towards their quarry and no sooner had the fly hit the water than the rod arched over.

It was exactly at this point where my experience of fly fishing thus far disengaged from what I was seeing on the television. Whenever I hooked my rainbow trout at Weir Wood Reservoir they would jump about a bit and maybe run a few yards and take some line, but never had one ever actually turned the reel handle! But this was different; the rod was arched over, all the slack line that had been at the angler's feet had gone through the butt ring in a flash and the reel handle was just blur as the fish tore off to the horizon. The fish, whatever it was, was obviously big, unlike my rainbows that averaged about a pound, but after a while the fish eventually stopped running. The angler then had to reel like crazy to keep up with the mystery fish as it ran at speed back towards him and in no time at all it was close to the boat. I wasn't totally sure at this point what exactly would happen next, but I guessed that they would try to land the fish in some way but no, the fish had different ideas and was soon heading, once again and at breakneck speed, back out to the horizon. The whole episode was replayed two more times before, finally, the angler in the well of the boat leaned over the side to lift the fish on board.

By now I was totally absorbed and looked on eagerly, waiting to see what manner of fish this would be as it was lifted aboard. It was clearly going to be a big one, but this couldn't have been further from the truth. The fish was not anywhere near as big as I had imaged and was about 4 pounds in weight. How could a fish of that size fight so hard? This was also when I heard the word "bonefish" for the first time. I was struck by how wonderful the fish

Anegada

looked and it was at that point I knew that I had to catch one. This was a future angling goal I had to fulfil.

Of course, having such an ambition is all well and good, but Southern England is not noted for its bonefishing and I guessed that it would probably turn out to be an expensive exercise. With a large mortgage, one young child and another soon to arrive, I decided to park the idea for a while but I knew I would return to it at a later stage.

The next time bonefishing came into my thoughts was in 1998. It was our 25th wedding anniversary and Sue and I were in Antigua and had hired a car and travelled out to see a local tourist attraction. This attraction involved a hole in a rocky outcrop where the sea was propelled into a plume of water and although it was a nice day out, my opinion at the time was that the spectacle wouldn't rate as one of the wonders of the world. As Sue and I approached the water spout we saw another couple walking towards us and we stopped for what turned out to be a fairly lengthy chat about holiday destinations. They mentioned how they liked to visit Virgin Gorda which is one of the British Virgin Islands in the Caribbean. This would eventually turn out to be another pivotal moment along the route to my first bonefish.

On returning home, I booked a holiday in Virgin Gorda and started to surf the net to find places of interest and this is where I first came across Anegada. The island of Anegada is, in fact, a small atoll about an hour's boat ride from Virgin Gorda. There were, I found out, bonefish to be caught around the island and, more importantly, a genuine bonefishing guide named Garfield lived there. As I said, this was a pivotal bonefishing moment for me and as soon as I knew I was going to be an hour's boat ride away from catching a bonefish everything kicked off. I bought a couple of saltwater fly rods, two reels, lines, clothing and all the other bits and pieces associated with bonefishing. Nowadays, as I write in 2011, this is very easy to do, but in the UK in 1998 this was more of a challenge, as bonefishing hardly ever got a mention in the angling press. Apart from just a few tackle shops that stocked some tackle that was suitable for saltwater fly fishing, finding the right equipment was difficult. Having said that, because this involved quite a lot of homework and determination, it was good fun and I felt a great sense of achievement as each critical item of kit and paraphernalia was acquired.

I also had to start learning about bonefishing; how do you catch them and what flies do you use? These were pressing questions that needed to be answered! My salvation was Dick Brown's excellent book *Fly Fishing for Bonefish* which I read from cover to cover several times, so that I had a fair idea of the importance of preparation before the trip, the way bonefish relate to different stages of the tide and how critical a stealthy approach would be. And then of course there was the need to understand what flies to use; I remember at the time feeling very confused about this and had made my mind up to leave any decision on fly selection to Garfield the guide.

Anegada

The holiday to the Virgin Islands couldn't come soon enough, I was more excited about this trip than any fishing I had done over the previous 30 years. This was because the fishing was going to be so different, not least because it would involve fly fishing in the sea. The other factor was the legendary fighting qualities of the bonefish which I had seen many years previously on the television programme and had read about in Dick Brown's book. Although I was becoming increasingly desperate to hook into a bonefish, I did find the prospect somewhat intimidating!

Eventually the holiday came around and Sue and I found ourselves staying in Biras Creek which is a very relaxing hotel on the small, lush island of Virgin Gorda. Prior to travelling I had done my homework and contacted Garfield to book a day with him to fish the flats on Anegada. The logistics for this had proved quite difficult as there was only one connection each week between Virgin Gorda and Anegada, which was by small boat, and if the weather was not good then it would be cancelled. This was the first time I would experience the link that always exists between bonefishing and the weather; something that I would face time and time again in future years. So, I would just have to keep my fingers crossed and hope for calm weather.

Having arrived in the British Virgin Islands at the weekend, the day with Garfield was arranged for the following Wednesday which meant I could get rid of any jet lag and be razor sharp to focus on the job at hand! It also gave me plenty of time to get all my gear together, which is always something I enjoy when on a bonefishing trip. However, when the special day arrived the weather did not look promising with grey cloud cover and a stiff breeze. There was a lot of discussion in the hotel about whether or not the boat would make the trip. After all the energy, preparation and expense I had so far put into trying to catch a bonefish, this was a very uncomfortable moment for me, but eventually the go-ahead was given and Sue and I boarded the small boat, destined to see Anegada and hopefully a bonefish for the first time!

The trip across to Anegada was pretty unpleasant, there was a decent swell and I guess that the boat crossing really had been touch-and-go, but finally the island came into view. This was not that easy as Anegada is only 12 miles long and, perhaps more importantly, just 28 feet at its highest point, so in a rough sea it only appears when you are a few hundred yards away. The island has just a few inhabitants, there is one small hotel, a jetty and a few other dwellings, but the overriding impression is of sand and mangrove with just the odd tree, so it's a very typical bonefishing destination.

Now that we had arrived I wasn't sure what would happen next. All the other passengers on the boat had disapeared to find a beach, so Sue and I sat outside the Anegada Reef Hotel drinking a Kalik and waiting for Garfield to arrive. This introduced me to yet another key aspect of bonefishing, which is the relaxed timekeeping that some guides seem to work to and for someone like me, who always turns up early for appointments, I find it particularly stressful. But we didn't have to wait too long, and I soon had my first glimpse of a bonefish skiff as Garfield sped into the bay and pulled up next to the jetty. The day and my bonefish journey was about to begin!

At this point it is worth remembering that booking a bonefish guide plus skiff for a day's fishing is not cheap and that the main point of the day is to fish. But, and it's a substantial but, there is far more to a day's bonefishing than just catching fish and, although this clearly applies to all forms of fishing, it is never more the case than when spending a day on the flats with a good guide. The ride in the skiff can often be worth the fee alone and a 30-minute high-speed jaunt as you weave between barely perceptible sandbars, past mangrove islands and over deep channels with the wind in your hair, is thoroughly exhilarating...and that's before you even get to where you are going! Once you arrive at your destination, if there isn't much wind, there is a wonderful silence and in this busy world we live in it is not often we experience true silence, where there isn't even the rustle of a leaf on a tree. I always savour that silence as I know that it is all too rare an event, even on a bonefish flat. Finally, there is the choice of either wading the flat or fishing from the skiff, but both styles give you the opportunity to just soak up the vista that can at times be simply overwhelming. And if you can catch a bonefish too, then life is pretty good.

Of course, on this particular day, neither Sue nor I had experienced any of this before and it was a revelation. The flats on Anegada run down the sea side of the island as opposed to the ocean side, and we headed off at speed to the far end so that we could then slowly pole back. As it was all very new to me I relied on Garfield to give me guidance and after asking him to select a suitable fly and getting a nod of approval about my rod, reel, line and leader, we commenced our first drift.

You hear the term bonefish flat but there is no one type of bonefish flat, even on the same island. Anegada's largest flat is a mixture of different colours made up of weed, marl and firm white sand at a variety of depths which gives a patchwork effect. Add to this the very strong wind, scudding clouds and high tide that we had on the day and it made spotting fish, for a novice like me, just impossible. In fact I didn't even know what to look for as we poled our way across the flat, but I tried to give the appearance that I knew what I was doing as we drifted for the first hour without seeing a thing.

We must have been a few minutes into our second drift when Garfield gave me very firm instructions that I should cast 50 feet at 11 o'clock and I remember feeling very inadequate and embarrassed as my line landed in a heap 20 feet away at about 12 o'clock. It was at this point that I became acutely aware that I had let Garfield down, as he had spent over an hour poling the boat in very windy and cloudy conditions looking for bonefish only for me to let all of his efforts go to waste. The rest of the day seemed to follow this pattern, with me never seeing a fish, but Garfield occasionally spotting some only for me to cast either too short, too long or in the wrong direction. To be fair to myself, the very strong wind and cloud cover made casting extremely difficult. There weren't many fish around and by mid-afternoon I had neither caught nor even seen my legendary quarry.

With only an hour or so left before the fishing day ended, the thought that I would soon have to get back to the jetty to get the return ferry, left me feeling a bit subdued. I had imagined the capture of my first bonefish in my mind many times over the past year, but I now felt like someone whose date hadn't turned up. After five hours of standing, interspersed with the odd bad cast, I was just going through the motions. The final minutes ticked by, the wind was starting to relax ready for the evening and, just when I thought my bonefish dream was to end in disappointment, Garfield once again told me the time and how far I should cast. For once my fly landed in the right place and after obeying Garfield's orders to wait I was given the go ahead to start retrieving.

It must have been on about the third or fourth pull back when suddenly everything went solid. At long last I had hooked my first bonefish and it was heading towards the mangroves! I remember, very vividly, watching the line that was once coiled on the deck, now zip at breakneck speed through the butt ring, the jolt as tight line hit the reel and, just as in the film, the reel handles were a blur. The bonefish must have gone a 100 yards or so and then it suddenly turned and I had to furiously rewind as the fish ran towards me. Then, just as quickly, it turned once again and was on another long run, but eventually the fish was 20 or so yards away. I was thinking how great it would be to just see and touch a bonefish for the first time, when it came off.

Someone who does not have any real affinity with angling would never understand what this feels like; after all it's only a fish, but to me it wasn't only a fish. It represented so much hard work and effort and a dream that for the time being would continue unfulfilled. On the journey back to Virgin Gorda I felt thoroughly miserable and although I tried to shake it off I knew that the feeling of disappointment would hang around until I caught my first bonefish – as surely I would!

Looking back on that first trip to Anegada, it only served to heighten my interest in bonefishing and I learnt over time that very strong winds, cloudy days and lost fish are all part of the sport – but I could have done without all three on the same day, first time out!

Chapter 2

Eleuthera

Eleuthera is an ideal place to try out and get a taste for bonefishing, as it is one of the few Bahamian out islands where it is easy to fish on your own rather than book a guide. There is little in the way of the organized guide programmes that you see on some of the other islands. The island of Eleuthera is just over 60 miles in length but only averages about 5 miles in width, which means that it is relatively simply to pull off the grandly named Queen's Highway, which runs up and down the island, and check out any likely looking beaches and flats for bones!

My initial visit to the island followed on from the Anegada trip, so I still had to catch my first bonefish. On the plane over from Nassau, coming in to land I could clearly see a large flats area close to the Governor's Harbour Airport which, not surprisingly, was named the airport flat. I was accompanied on the trip by Trevor Ashton, an old friend. We were both excited about the prospect of catching bonefish and had been talking the trip up for months, buying loads of bonefish stuff and discussing tactics. The trip had been organized through Carol and Graham Pepler who ran Bonefish Adventure in Christchurch, Dorset. The deal was that we would stay in the Rainbow Inn, be given a car, a map and some bonefishing instruction. We would then be left alone, if we so wished, to explore the island and hopefully to catch some bones which sounded great.

What we hadn't planned for was Hurricane Floyd. The lead up to the trip had been very much touch-and-go as Floyd moved through the Bahamas towards Florida, creating havoc and destruction along the way. Although we had managed to miss the hurricane by a couple of weeks, flights to Eleuthera had only resumed three days before our departure date. When we finally touched down on the island the destruction was plain to see: boats were in trees a 100 yards from the shore, many buildings had roofs torn off and were badly damaged and all of the roads close to the shore had sections completely destroyed. What little road remained had massive potholes from which there would be no easy escape!

However, none of this mattered as we had arrived and, just as importantly, so had our gear. We were ready to fish and were pleased to meet Carol at the airport. As is always the case in the Bahamas, I soon found myself drinking an ice cold Kalik within minutes of getting off the plane; a tradition that continues thankfully to this day.

"What do you guys want to do," Carol asked, "go straight to the hotel or fish now?" And so we fished. The nearest flat was the airport flat which took us all of five minutes to drive to. The weather, unlike the previous few weeks, was now pretty good and it was pleasantly warm and sunny with just a light wind. The tide was in, which meant that if we were going to see any bonefish then, as I learnt later, they would be in tight schools. We wandered along the beach, amongst the flotsam and jetsam, scanning the water and then, as if by magic, along came a school of bonefish close to the shoreline. This was my first experience of actually seeing bonefish and also my first experience of the bonefish shakes which turns legs to jelly and destroys the ability to cast! But cast I did and I caught my first ever bonefish and, like everyone else who has done the same thing, it is a never to be forgotten experience. The fish wasn't big, maybe a couple pounds, but of course at that stage in my bonefishing career size wasn't that important – just catching one was the main thing. However, despite being just a 2-pounder it was big enough to do a proper bonefish run that I could bore people with back home. Perhaps, more importantly, it also released me from the heartache of losing the Anegada fish and fulfilled a 20-year ambition, so what more could I ask for. In fact, there was one more thing, which was that Trevor would also catch his first bonefish and this he did. We had both fulfilled an ambition – what a great start to a week's fishing. The Kaliks would flow that evening!

The following morning, Trevor and I had concluded that we were, indeed, bonefishing experts and had decided to set off on our own. Our car was a huge America model which I believe was a Chevrolet, although I am not totally sure, however, big and American it surely was. It was also very old, but did work which was the main thing and in the week that followed I enjoyed driving around on Eleuthera's intermittent and challenging roads almost as much as the fishing. Some of the potholes were a foot deep and only once did we manage to find ourselves in one which resulted, not surprisingly, in a puncture.

The fishing on Eleuthera, as with the most of the Bahamian out islands, can be done on the Atlantic Ocean side or the Bahamian Sea side of the island. The sea side is generally an easier affair on Eleuthera and most of the flats and beaches that lend themselves to bone fishing are on that side of the island. The airport flat, following our early success, was an obvious hotspot that we targeted, but apart from one other bonefish we never repeated the double hook up of that first day. We also fished Ten Bay and, although there were rumours that the beach had been netted and there were no bonefish left, I did catch one which was encouraging.

Trevor and I also fished Hatchet Bay and Palmetto Point and caught bonefish from both places. Hatchet Bay is an enchanting spot, the small settlement is set in a deep, sheltered bay that is hidden from the prevailing winds. There is an obliging school of bonefish living in the area and we found them not too difficult to catch. Palmetto Point was a much larger expanse of wading flat that contained better than average-sized bonefish and Trevor landed one at around the 4-pound mark from here, which is a good-sized fish for Eleuthera.

Another productive area that I found interesting to fish was Balara Bay, also on the sea side, which gave us the most exciting fishing of the week. The route to the bay is over a very rough track and, not surprisingly, our big Chevrolet had to be abandoned part way down with the rest of the journey on foot. On our first visit to Balara, as Trevor and I emerged from the dense undergrowth that hugged the shoreline, we were hit full in the face by a howling onshore wind. The obvious remnants of Hurricane Floyd, it had been building as the week went on, so fishing where we were standing wasn't an option.

To our left was a large bay that was slightly sheltered from the strong wind. This gave the best chance of some productive fishing, so after a further walk along the shore line I waded into the water, knee deep amongst some dark green weed that had accumulated close to the shore. It was impossible to see into the water, which was very cloudy as it had been stirred up by the strong wind. I put on a size 2 chartreuse Clouser Minnow and managed, despite the wind, to cast it out 15 yards. Sight fishing it certainly wasn't. It felt more like bank fishing for rainbow trout at Grafham Water back in the UK rather than bonefishing, but the whole set-up had that fishy feeling. Something was telling me that there was a chance of a fish of some sort.

That first cast lasted just two pulls and then there was a vicious tug followed by slackness. I was surprised that I had failed to hook up with whatever had taken the fly, but on checking my leader I found the fly was no longer there. I commented to Trevor that maybe something with teeth, perhaps a barracuda, had grabbed my fly. Almost at that moment his rod arched over and he was into something that behaved just like a bonefish as it made a spectacular first run, and sure enough he landed a nice one of about 4 pounds. So they were out there and feeding!

Apart from the capture of this first bonefish from Balara, the other interesting thing was that the weed I was standing in kept moving and I suddenly realized that the weed was, in fact, a huge shoal of many thousands of small, dark green fry, which was clearly what the bonefish were interested in and, of course, the clouser was an ideal pattern to use. Amazingly I dropped the clouser under the rod tip into the shoal of fry and immediately had another vicious take from a bonefish only for it to come off. It did illustrate that bonefish do lose their inhibitions when there is a plentiful food source available and the weather is so rough that it cushions their senses. In the end I did catch a bonefish which at four and a half pounds was easily my biggest to date and Trevor also picked up another but, inevitably in the strengthening wind, it became impossible to cast, so we reluctantly made our way back to find our abandoned car. But fishing under the leaden sky, with the relentless wind, the waves and the fry, combined with catching the bonefish left me with one of those lasting fishing memories.

What Trevor and I didn't realize was that the strong wind would remain for the rest of the week, which made the fishing extremely difficult. Since then I have come to understand that strong winds are, for much of the time, synonymous with bonefishing and that being capable of accurately casting the required distance in conditions that aren't ideal is key to consistent success.

The other overriding memory for me during that week was fishing Savannah Sound, on the ocean side of the island, which is sheltered from the worst excesses of the wind and waves, by Windemere Island. This area isn't a creek or a flat, but a large expanse of sandy bottom with a fair amount of weed growth. After a number of visits to Savannah Sound it became apparent that the best way to fish it was to get there at low tide and position yourself on one of the sand channels waiting for the tide and bonefish to come in together, which they surely do.

What Savannah taught me most in my formative stage as a bonefisher, is the importance of good knots, line and leaders. If this combination isn't right, it will cost you fish which is what happened to me. I'm not going to elaborate on this except to say that I got broken up by four of the five fish I hooked on my first visit to Savannah. As a result, I now use tapered 13-pound leaders for nearly all my bone fishing and have as few knots as possible; only begrudgingly will I add a tippet to my leader. Of course, at Savannah, I hadn't yet worked this out and paid the cost through too many lost fish. But this is how you learn!

The other thing I learnt, or should I say became apparent to me, was how you see bonefish when it is very windy and the surface of the water is broken up by waves. I noticed that although the surface of the water was disturbed there was a uniformity of light pattern to this disturbance. Any bonefish, although difficult to spot, would subtly change this light pattern as they moved about and they suddenly became more visible. Once I realized this I found it easier to spot bonefish and get more hook ups but, as mentioned, I didn't land many on that first day!

Apart from my brief visit to Anegada, this was my first genuine foray into bonefishing and although Trevor and I didn't catch many bonefish during the week, it did give us a glimpse of what bonefishing is about. I remember being particularly pleased about spotting fish and fishing without a guide heightens your ability to do this. There isn't anyone there to do it for you and if you don't see the fish you simply will not catch. In fact, thinking about it now, that week on Eleuthera spent fishing on my own really did hammer home all the things I didn't know about bonefishing or needed to improve upon. My progress as a bonefisher was ultimately accelerated because of this.

Governor's Harbour was also a great place to practice fish spotting, as the high harbour wall which edges the bay gives a great vantage point from which to spot fish. Trevor and I would stop off there on most days as we travelled up and down the island and catch the odd bonefish. There is, however, a large school of bonefish-sized mullet

Eleuthera

that kept me fooled for a good part of the week and they are pretty much uncatchable so beware!

I also had my first glimpse of bonefish behaviour in relation to the various stages of the tide and learnt how critical this was to success. I started to understand how, at high water, they would form into tight schools. Then they would gradually disperse as the tide began to ebb until, when there was hardly any water to cover their backs, they would suddenly scatter across a flat and become tailing fish, either as individuals or in groups of two or three fish.

Thinking back, I didn't manage to catch a tailing bonefish during my first week on Eleuthera, but certainly realized I wanted to and made sure this was would be one of my aims as I planned the next trip.

In those early bonefishing days I was a bit like a kid in a sweet shop, as there were so many destinations to try out. The lure of other places kept me away from Eleuthera until several years later when Sue and I decided to take our summer holiday there and also on Harbour Island which is just off the northern tip of Eleuthera. Unlike my previous trip, there weren't any hurricanes and the weather was pretty much perfect the whole week. As before, we stayed in the Rainbow Inn but this time had a very modern four-wheel drive vehicle that, whilst not being as much fun as the old Chevrolet, was a lot more reliable!

Funnily enough, I failed to catch a single bonefish in any of the hot spots that I fished during the first visit and I failed to even spot a single fish at Savannah, Palmetto

Point or Balara, which was a worry and I suspected some netting had been going on. This is always a hazard where there isn't an advanced guide programme on an island. I suspect this wouldn't happen so much on other Bahamian islands, such as Andros, where the local economy depends so much on bonefishing.

However, one place that definitely had plenty of bonefish was Hatchet Bay and there was a huge school in and around the bay all week which gave me some excellent catches, although they were typical Eleuthera bonefish at around the 2- to 3-pound mark. I remember fishing early one Sunday morning when a service was being held in the small church by the bay. It was thoroughly enchanting listening to the hymn singing whilst bonefishing!

Looking back on my two trips to Eleuthera I would say I enjoyed them as much as anywhere I have bonefished. The island is not commercialized and is very relaxed which lends itself to the do-it-yourself style of bonefishing. The average size of bonefish is smaller than on some of the other islands in the Bahamas, but that somehow doesn't matter when you are the only one making the decisions about where and how you are going to fish. And of course you also have to do all the fish spotting yourself. It's because of these two reasons I know I will be returning to Eleuthera yet again at some time in the future.

Chapter 3

Los Roques

A week's bonefishing is always, for me, an enjoyable experience, but there will be trips which will be rewarding for reasons other than just the fishing, and my first visit to Los Roques fell into this category. Trevor and I had decided to go there mostly on the back of a bonefishing video that I had bought that contained a fair bit of action from Los Roques. There wasn't much of a story line, it involved a bloke and a girl in very tight fitting bonefish shorts catching loads of bonefish. Thinking back, the people in the video must have been fishing a mud but they were certainly catching plenty of fish and some good-sized ones too, which was enough to persuade Trevor and me that Los Roques was worth a try!

Los Roques lies just off the north coast of Venezuela and like many bonefish destinations is an atoll, a small lagoon ringed by islands the largest of which, with little imagination, is named Grand Roques. However, unlike the Bahamas where the out islands can be reached on the same day of departure from Heathrow, this was my

A Bonefishing Journey

first experience of a two-day journey to get to a bonefish destination. This is something I have since learnt to avoid as it increases cost and reduces fishing time. The flight over from the UK was trouble-free but my overriding memory of Caracas Airport was of being met by a mass of taxi drivers, all eager to relieve me of as much money as possible. Although I felt this would inevitably happen, I said to Trevor that we should retain an element of control and at least select the taxi driver who was going to rip us off, which we did.

The connecting flight to Los Roques was the next day so we had arranged to stay overnight in Caracas and fly out the following morning. The airport is at least a 45-minute journey from Caracas city centre and is as far, metaphorically speaking, as you can get from a trip round the M25 towards Heathrow. The journey was a real experience as the car we were travelling in had just about every warning light shining like a beacon on the dashboard, and those that weren't probably had bulbs that had blown. With no air conditioning all the windows were down, and I made the mistake of not holding my breath as we entered the first of a number of very long tunnels along the route to Caracas, all of which were filled with dense, acrid, black, car smoke. A couple of other things struck me on the journey; the first was that the whole highway just went up and down due to a combination of subsidence and perhaps the tarmac melting in the heat. This gave a ride that was reminiscent of a gentle roller coaster. The other thing was

Los Roques

that the hillsides adjacent to the highway were covered in an assortment of shanty towns. Every so often a huge gap of wasteland would appear on the hillside. Presumably the result of mud slides on the steep slopes which caused the dwellings to simply move down the hill. It's at times like this that the differences between one part of the world and another hits home – life looked pretty tough for the people on the hillside.

By total contrast Trevor and I arrived at our hotel, the Hilton, to be greeted by a very large doorman. The hotel was an oasis of opulence and calm in amongst the hustle and bustle of Caracas and as the taxi pulled up the doorman leaned in and asked us how much the driver had quoted. "$80." I said. "Give him $20." replied the doorman, so we paid the unhappy driver his $20 and tipped the doorman the same – a saving of $40!

The following morning we had the same routine in reverse as we made our way back out to the airport to catch an internal flight to Los Roques but, as we knew we wouldn't have a friendly doorman to welcome us when we arrived at the terminal, we successfully negotiated $40 for the ride up front. Maybe it's just me, but I find collecting these internal flights very stressful, mainly because there can sometimes be a complete lack urgency by flight staff and quite often there is no flight staff at all until the last minute, as was evident on this particular morning. And of course, if you don't speak the local language, as in my case, it just goes to further heighten the tension.

Eventually someone did arrive at the check-in desk and, after clearing up some initial confusion about whether Trevor and I were on the flight list, we found ourselves sharing the waiting room with a number of local people and chickens in equal numbers. I wasn't quite sure what plane to expect and we sat in the waiting area for what must have been a couple of hours watching a procession of small, modern looking planes landing. However, I wasn't surprised by the lack of a boarding call and I had a feeling that I shouldn't expect anything too special. Eventually an old green Douglas DC-3 came into view and my heart sank. The DC-3s had been used extensively in the Second World War and I remembered them well from watching old, Second World War films. This one looked as if it had seen plenty of action. My seat was next to the emergency exit by the wing and because of an ill-fitting door the exhaust fumes were blasted into the passenger compartment. I was also intrigued to see that all the backs to the passenger seats were broken and instead of being upright they were permanently in the reclined position. I was just pleased that it wasn't a transatlantic flight! The other interesting point was that, as the door was open to the flight deck, I could clearly see that water was entering the cabin above the pilot's head due to the heavy rain outside. The stewardess was keeping the water off the pilot using a box of tissues. However, despite all of these shortcomings we were still treated to the safety presentation by the stewardess.

Los Roques

Although all of this was a bit unnerving, and added an element of spice to the short flight, I was relieved when we touched down on Grand Roque. As is usually the case, we were met by our host Miguel and we were soon in his boat heading for Rasque Island, which is a short 10-minute ride away. Miguel was a Venezuelan and lived on the island with his girlfriend. The island was straight out of *Robinson Crusoe* and, apart from the mosquitoes, was an idyllic spot to have as our base for the week. It was even possible to get up and wander just a few yards to the sea and catch a bonefish before breakfast!

On my previous two bonefishing trips I had become used to fishing flats of one sort or another, but the fishing at Los Roques was completely different to anything I had experienced before. This tore up my blueprint that I had assumed could be applied to anywhere where there were bonefish. The most obvious surprise was that most of the fishing Trevor and I did that week was from beaches which often shelved into quite deep water, certainly far too deep to wade in to. There were flats, but once again they were different from those on Eleuthera and Anegada and instead of being made up of clear light sand or marl they were often covered in luxuriant weed growth and in particular, turtle grass. This last point proved a real challenge to me because I found fish spotting particularly difficult, especially when it was windy, which it often was. I also hadn't, at that point in my bonefishing learning cycle, understood the importance of "nervous water", and how to spot it. I knew it existed as I had already read plenty about it, but my impression was that it would be pretty obvious to spot. I had no idea at the time that nervous water can be a hardly perceptible occurrence that can be so slight that you wonder why your focus is drawn to some minute change in the pattern of surface water. Ironically, it is this ability to read movements under the water that are betrayed on the surface that can be the difference between a good and not so good day's fishing. The bonefisher who masters this craft will be all the more successful as a result.

The fishing on Los Roques was tough but interesting, and Trevor and I spent the week being ferried about by Miguel and his voluptuous girl friend who wore the smallest of bikinis all of the time! We were taken to a variety of spots and would mostly spend our time slowly walking along the beaches spotting and casting to bonefish. Like the previous two bonefishing trips, the weather played its part and we were told that the tides were particularly high, due to El Niño. This meant that the waves on to the beaches were also high, resulting in cloudy water that made sight fishing just that more difficult.

The most productive beaches by far were those on Grand Roque which were at the end of the runway and adjacent to it. The beach at the far end of the runway was a highly entertaining place to fish and Trevor nearly lost his head to low flying planes on a couple of occasions – it was so easy to become totally absorbed in the fishing to such an extent that the planes coming down the runway were simply forgotten about.

The end of runway beach was the most untypical bonefish spot imaginable. It was deep, so wading was completely out of the question, there were big waves and the water was so cloudy that there was little chance of sight fishing. In all honesty, I probably would never have fished there except that whilst walking along the beach I saw shoals of small glass minnows leaping out of the water close to the shore in amongst the murky waves. I then had a speculative cast with a Clouser Minnow and caught a bonefish. This really grabbed my attention! The takes when they came were truly rod wrenching and the fishing was great fun, but so unlike the bonefishing I had previously experienced. However, this was just another example of how varied bonefishing can be. Since that day I have never neglected beaches and have had some really good fish as a result, so ignore beaches at your cost.

The technique on the runway beach was to walk along it scanning the water and looking for the minnows to show themselves, which they did when they were being harassed by the bonefish. Usually this was about 20 yards offshore which meant a fairly demanding cast if the wind was in your face, as it often was. It was interesting to note that the depth of water this far out was about 6 feet, but the bonefish would happily feed in amongst the surface waves whilst chasing the glass minnows and it was not uncommon to see the bonefish leap clear of the water.

The flat that ran alongside the runway was slightly shallower and more sheltered from the wind and the water was clearer as a result. This meant that sight fishing and wading was possible albeit in waist-deep water. The bonefish were still feeding on glass minnows but, unlike the majority of bonefish that feed hard on the bottom, these fish would be chasing the fry in mid-water and would often swirl at the surface as they chased their quarry. This led to some really exciting fishing where it was possible to cast a Clouser Minnow close to a hunting bonefish and see it veer off course and take the fly. In fact, I had one bonefish take the fly literally 2 feet in front of where I was standing and it was an incredible experience to watch the fish inhale the fly at such close quarters.

Another fishing area that I found captivating was around the lobster fisherman's hut, which is a shack-like wooden building that had been erected right in the middle of a huge turtle grass flat. This area is well known as being a good bonefish spot and there are plenty of bonefish to be caught here although, if truth be known, I should have caught more than I did. There were good-sized shoals present, but because of the turtle grass I spooked far too many bonefish, although I did catch a few. One method that seemed to work well there was to cast a small crab pattern on to one of the sandy patches near the fisherman's hut and just leave it stationary rather than moving it. The bonefish preferred it that way whereas they would often ignore the fly if it was stripped back. I have found a stationary fly very effective at other destinations, especially on fish that are easily spooked and is a tactic I now regularly employ.

Fly selection for Los Roques was another surprise to me. On my trip to Anegada I had no preconceived ideas about what fly to use and was happy to let my guide pick the fly for me, but following the trip to Eleuthera I was convinced that any of the usual shrimp type patterns would work equally well. However, this was simply not the case at Los Roques where the majority of the bonefish I caught were on the Clouser Minnow with the remainder coming to the crab pattern. The Clouser Minnow worked because the fish here were preoccupied fry feeders and the Clouser was the ideal representation which proved deadly when stripped fast anywhere near a bonefish.

What I did find important, however, was the colour of the Clouser: a white one with a dark green back proved to be far more effective than the more usual chartreuse pattern that I have used with some success elsewhere. Presumably, the dark green backed version was a closer match to the fry the bonefish were eating, but the colour certainly worked. When I arrived at Los Roques I only had a couple of Clousers with the dark green backs and they lasted just a day or two. Fortunately, both Trevor and I always bring a fly tying vice plus some staple materials, so between us we had the necessary ingredients to tie up plenty of the dark green Clousers that would see us through to the end of the week.

The other productive fly, as I said, was a crab pattern. I had bought some very realistic crab patterns from Farlows in London prior to the trip and the bonefish seemed to like them, especially smallish ones tied on a size 6. What both the Clouser and the crab pattern had in common was that they were clearly representing what the bonefish were eating and, unlike the Eleuthera fish that would happily take moving flies that were only vaguely reminiscent of something edible, the Los Roques fish wanted exactly what they were eating and presented to them at the right speed. This was stripped fast in mid-water with the Clouser and stationary when using the crab.

This new experience with saltwater fly selection, where it was important to "match the hatch" so to speak, was a great lesson for me and has shaped my fly selection ever since. It doesn't mean to say that the fly has to mirror the bonefishes' food item in every detail, but shape, colour, size and movement are, collectively, very important.

The weather during the week was difficult and Miguel continually blamed El Niño for the ever-present cloudy sky and high tides. Now, looking back and having had the luxury and experience of many other bonefish trips, the weather wasn't that untypical when compared to what is normally encountered during a week's bonefishing. The high tide could also have been managed better if I had bothered to consult some tide tables, but of course at that moment in my bonefishing evolution, although I knew tides were important in bonefishing, I didn't realize how important. It was this trip to Los Roques that instilled in me the need to marry the correct tides with the destination – something which has stayed with me ever since.

One particular event relating to the weather that does hold in the memory was encountering a very heavy tropical rainstorm for the first time whilst fishing, which was an experience. Trevor and I were fishing a far-off flat that was close to the reef. The weather was sunny and we had both caught bonefish. On the edge of the reef was what looked from afar like a Spanish galleon that had run aground but, of course, once close up it was only an old fishing boat, but it gave the flat an air of mystery.

I was fishing close to the wreck and was a good long wade away from our boat which was parked up on the far edge of the flat. About midday I noticed a very dark cloud system on the horizon, but I didn't take too much notice of it as it was far-off and I continued to fish. The next time I looked up it wasn't so far away but was moving to the right, so I was reasonably comfortable that it would miss us, although it was close enough to clearly see very heavy rain the likes of which you don't get in the UK.

There were one or two bonefish about so I carried on fishing keeping a constant watch on the cloud system, but within minutes the ever deepening black cloud system had turned direction and was almost upon us. I shouted to warn Trevor and we both headed back to the boat at top wading speed, but we didn't stand a chance and the torrential rain hit us when we had a couple of hundred yards still to go. What surprised me was that the rain was absolutely freezing, which coming from England, I didn't expect in the tropics. We finally made it to the boat, but were shivering with cold by then, so opted to just sit on the flat up to our necks in sea water as this was clearly the warmest option. The thing that surprised me was that visibility, whilst in the storm, was just a few yards, such was the ferocity of the rain!

Once again, this was another learning experience and since then not only do I always take along my heavy Gore-Tex wading jacket, but also a lightweight, single layer rain jacket that folds up easily into a bum bag which I use whilst wading. This light jacket has saved me from getting wet and cold many times.

Looking back on that trip, my overriding memory of Los Roques was the size of the bonefish as it was my first experience of catching, and losing, really good-sized bonefish, and by that I mean fish of 5 pounds and upwards. My biggest fish of the week was about 7 pounds and I remember the blistering initial run at speed and experiencing for the first time the associated concern that I might run out of backing. On Eleuthera, the fish were much smaller and less intimidating, which was probably ideal for a bonefishing novice as I was at the time, but the fish from Los Roques were real man-sized bonefish that illustrated why so many people are captivated by the sport.

So, as with all bonefishing trips, this one to Los Roques came and went all too quickly. It gave me a completely different take on the bonefishing I had so far experienced and introduced me to other facets of the sport that I would need to understand and master if I was to feel really competent in what I was doing. My next trip would give me the chance to put it into practice.

Chapter 4

Long Island

Looking at a map of the Bahamas, Long Island looks very similar to Eleuthera as it is about the same size and shape being long and thin. My first trip there was with Sue and we had booked a week at the Stella Maris hotel which was a delightful place to stay and relax. As I was with Sue I knew I wouldn't be able to fish every day, but I would still be able to get in a couple of days fishing along with some early morning sessions before breakfast which might just possibly stretch to lunch!

As with all bonefish trips I touched down on the hotel airstrip with a head full of preconceptions. These were mostly centred on the fishing being much the same as I had experienced on Eleuthera, simply because of the similarity in shape and the close proximity of the two islands. Like many Bahamian islands the main road on Long Island is known as the Queen's Highway and I had the firmly fixed idea that there would be plenty of wadeable flats just a short stroll from the road, as there were in Eleuthera, but this proved to be anything but the case. And as far as

Long Island

utilizing the services of a local guide were concerned, I hadn't even given it a thought.

Over the course of the week Sue and I did quite a bit of exploring on the island, which is always a worthwhile exercise from a fishing point of view. It soon became apparent that the fishing on Long Island can be split roughly into three main areas with each offering a different bonefishing experience. There are good-sized flats, some at the north of the island and others a decent skiff ride off the western shoreline. There are some bays and a little shore fishing, but much of this is not easily accessible and involves a lengthy walk through mangroves and goo before you eventually realize that you need a guide and a skiff! Finally, there is the Deadman's Caye area which, although it gives the impression of looking like normal flats, is in fact flooded salt workings but the area does, nevertheless, offer excellent bonefishing.

A look through my fishing diary tells me that I have had three trips to Long Island, but the first trip there was probably the most pivotal in the process of moving me on from the novice stage into a bonefisher who felt like they had some idea and purpose to what they were doing. It also introduced me to the importance of fishing with a really excellent guide.

The first couple of days were spent trying to locate some do-it-yourself bonefishing. A mile or so from the hotel was Adderley's Bay and, taking advantage of the free bikes that were available to hotel guests, Sue and I would ride to the bay and fish there when the tide was right. This was great fun, especially on the way there as it was all downhill, but I caught only one bonefish. I did, however, see plenty of bonefish but the depth and soft marl bottom prevented me from wading out to them. The uphill ride back at midday was pretty tough, too, and required a cool beer or two to fully recover. So, although the biking sessions were good fun I needed another plan if I was going to catch bonefish in any number.

I then spent a further day driving up and down the Queen's Highway looking for accessible wade fishing, but after a few abortive attempts, where I finished up tired and muddy from walking through mangroves, I finally came to the conclusion that I would need a guide. Fortunately for me, the Stella Maris hotel had a really excellent guide in Docky Smith. Having now fished with many guides from different locations I am now very aware that guides differ greatly in their local fishing knowledge, angling ability, enthusiasm and companionship. Docky ticked all of these boxes and was extremely professional in his whole approach to bonefish guiding. However, he had one other attribute that he shared with all the really good guides in that he was a very proficient coach and on the first day I spent with Docky my ability to see fish, cast and strip strike all improved markedly. It also illustrated the importance of calling on the skills and experience of a guide when bonefishing, as it can get you up and running and catching fish far quicker than if you tried it yourself.

Long Island

On that first trip I had a couple of days out with Docky and we fished Adderley's Bay where I caught some of the bonefish I had seen on the biking sessions. We also fished some of the creeks at the top of the island. There were good numbers of bonefish present in the creeks and much of the fishing was wading over hard, white sand which is always rewarding and enjoyable. Both days with Docky were productive and on one of them I managed to catch seven fish which, as this was the most I had ever taken in one day, made me feel as if I was starting to become a reasonably proficient bonefisher, but of course since then I have had many other days that have brought me back down to earth!

However, a couple of days' fishing, plus some early morning two-hour sessions, were never going to give me a complete picture of the fishing on the island and it wasn't until my next trip the following year that I felt I really got to know the island from a bonefishing point of view. Like so many bonefish trips, there was considerable uncertainty about whether I would actually get to Long Island. The trip was planned for October, but the World Trade Center in New York had tragically been destroyed on September 11th and this severely disrupted world airlines for some time. And then, just when the airlines were returning to normal schedules, Hurricane Michelle hit the Bahamas and caused further cancellations to flights.

In the end I did, just, make it to Long Island and Trevor, Phil and I touched down safely on the landing strip at Stella

Maris late on a Wednesday afternoon. We were greeted by the hotel welcoming committee on the runway with trays of rum punch! What a great start to a week's fishing.

Trevor had, of course, fished before on Eleuthera and Los Roques but Phil, who was a competent fly fisherman, had not previously bonefished so this was a new experience for him. As with Eleuthera, we hired another large American car and the first couple of days were pretty much wasted as we spent time exploring the south of the island. As with my previous trip, we failed to locate any easily accessible wadeable flats due to the extensive mangroves that line the shore, so do-it-yourself fishing wasn't going to be an option. We did, however, stumble across Deadman's Caye for the first time and could clearly see that it had real potential, so we booked two guides for the following day. The arrangement was that Colin Cartwright would guide for Trevor and me at Deadman's Caye and that Phil would have a day's fishing with Docky in the north of the island. Not surprisingly, we immediately gained access to excellent fishing and all caught bonefish that day.

The fishing during the remainder of the week was very good and easily my best bonefishing so far. I had more fish and bigger fish than in previous trips. As is always the case on any fishing trip there were a couple things that really stood out for me. The first was when Phil and I fished an area known as Turtle Rock. The rock lies way off the island to the west and involves a lengthy skiff journey that takes about 45 minutes. Fortunately, on the day that

Long Island

Phil and I made the trip, the sea was like a millpond which was a relief as I wouldn't want to make the journey in rough weather. The rock itself took a bit of finding, as at high tide it barely showed above the surface of the water and was only about 15 feet in length when we arrived there. As we tossed the anchor into water about 3-feet deep we were greeted by a primordial scene that I will never forget. A huge gathering of bonefish, containing many thousands packed into a very tight shoal, were just off the rock and it was easy to see why, as they were circled by half a dozen big lemon sharks plus two extremely large barracuda. We stood in the skiff and watched intently as every so often mayhem would break out when one of the waiting predators lunged into the shoal to make a kill. This was a truly fascinating scene and one that I had never witnessed before.

Phil and I sat patiently in the boat for an hour or so waiting for the tide to drop to a point where it was no longer possible for the sharks and barracudas to remain where they were. We did try at one stage to get out of the boat so that we could have a go for the bonefish, but the water was still too deep and the lemon sharks started to take too much of an interest in us which meant we had to make a rapid retreat to the boat.

I am always amazed by how quickly things can change at a certain stage of the tide. Within just a few minutes the tide had dropped and the bonefish shoal had broken up and dispersed across, what was now, a very big flat that stretched 360 degrees to the horizon. Not only that, but these were genuine tailing bonefish, just as I had read about in the books and it was every bit as exciting as described. At long last I was going to get a chance to fish for some genuine tailing bonefish.

It is fair to say that the next three hours fishing was, without a doubt, the most exciting, challenging and rewarding bonefishing I had ever experienced. It was blisteringly hot and there was not a breath of wind, so I was surrounded by that total silence. To able kneel down in just a few inches of water and cast to tailing fish little more than a rod length away was captivating – this was bonefishing as good as it gets. At one point I even had an osprey swoop down and try and catch a feeding bonefish right in front of me. It missed the fish, but it certainly spooked the shoal! And finally, just to cap things off, I caught my biggest bonefish thus far. It was 7½ pounds and really took off at an incredible speed in the shallow water. It was the first time I had experienced how fast and how far a decent-sized bonefish will run.

Our time at Turtle Rock ended all too quickly as a combination of the rising tide and failing light meant we had to head back. That was, and still is, the only time I have fished Turtle Rock and part of me wants to go back but something else tells me to quit while I am ahead and stick with the memory of a very special few hours fishing.

The second key memory was about failing to catch a fish rather than catching one. I was out with Docky fishing one of the large creeks in the north of the island. The weather was pretty good, but by lunchtime we hadn't caught or even seen a bonefish, which was odd. We then motored out of the creek and found out why. The bonefish were shoaled up and surround by maybe 20 sharks, but unlike Turtle Rock, the sharks were some distance from the shoal and were just slowly circling it. With the bonefish shoal in 6 or 7 feet of water, fishing for them wasn't an option so we move off contemplating the next move.

We had only just got back on to the shallower water when we spotted a biggish ray with two large permit on its tail. This was the first time I had seen a permit and they looked huge compared to bonefish. Docky estimated both fish were 30 pounds plus as we eagerly slid over the side of the skiff to try and catch one. To cut a very long story short, we must have followed the permit for about half a mile before we hit a channel that was too deep to wade and had to give up. During the long wade I continually put my crab pattern on or very close to the back of the ray. On three occasions one of the permit appeared to go down on the fly and on three occasions I strip struck into thin air! I guess the permit lived up to their legendary status, but the episode only fuelled my desire to catch one at some point.

The rest of our fishing took place at Deadman's Caye which is an interesting and at times bizarre place to bonefish, as in some places it is a bit like fishing in a petrified forest. When the salt workings were operating the high level of salinity killed off large swathes of the mangroves, but the remnants still remain in the form of black stumps that stick out of the water. This makes playing bonefish highly entertaining, as the fly line will often wrap itself around the stumps and the required technique here is to run after the bonefish unhooking the fly line as you go. Despite this new challenge, we all became adept at this and landed most of the bonefish we hooked. I found the bonefishing in Deadman's Caye interesting as it was mostly wading for small pods of bonefish, with plenty of opportunity to cast at tailing fish. It was also enjoyable to fish with Colin as he had a great understanding of that area of the island.

Something that I found particularly fascinating was the coordinated way in which the bonefish at Deadman's Caye would feed. A typical shoal of around a dozen fish would line up next to each other, with perhaps a couple of feet between each fish, and then move forward in a line slowly feeding as they went. They would cover about 10 yards before scattering, only to reform again, except this time they would be either to the right or left from where they originally started, depending on which way the tide was moving. In effect they were working together and feeding in a zigzag fashion and would continue to do this throughout the best period of the tide.

From an angler's point of view it was easy to use this behaviour to my advantage. I would wait until they had finished feeding in a line and then cast as they were scattering to reform the line. Because they were swimming away from me, they were unaware of the cast and it was simply a matter of leaving the fly stationary on the bottom and wait for the next line of bonefish to approach it. A couple of short pulls at the appropriate time would invariably result in a hooked bonefish. Since then I have seen bonefish do this in other locations, especially when they are in smallish shoals.

Up until Long Island my use and understanding of bonefish flies was surrounded by uncertainty, but the fishing experience there firmly cemented my belief in the Gotcha as a superb bonefish fly, and I used the pattern pretty much to the exclusion of everything else. For the most part I was fishing over hard, light sand so it was always going to be the perfect fly. I did use other flies, but nothing came close to the Gotcha when it came to catching bonefish. What I also realized about the Gotcha was that the shop-bought versions only ever came in one weight and to get the most out of the pattern I needed a selection of different sizes and, just as importantly, weights. As a result I spent more time at the fly tying vice on Long Island than I had on other trips and tied up a selection of differently weighted Gotchas which paid dividends.

As far as bonefishing destinations are concerned, Long Island will always be on my list of places to go. It does have lodges and organized trips, but like many of the Bahamian out islands it also has some excellent independent guides who will cater for anglers fishing on their own. It is also possible to rent accommodation that can be used as a base for fishing, which is what Trevor, Phil and I did on our last trip there. And, of course, it is home to large populations of good-sized bonefish in a variety of habitats which provide really excellent fishing. What more could you ask for.

Chapter 5

Virgin Gorda

Virgin Gorda is not normally associated with being a bonefish destination, but it does produce bonefish and they can be very large. In fact the biggest bonefish I ever saw was in Virgin Gorda, but more of that later. One of the British Virgin Islands, Virgin Gorda is hilly and rocky and not very big. It is also one of the most unlikely places you would expect to find bonefish!

My first visit there was when I fished nearby Anegada but Sue and I returned once again the following year. I hadn't expected to see bonefish on the island simply because there were no flats to speak of and the rocky terrain, so it appeared, just shelved off into deep water. There were, however, some rocky flats and a small number of sandy beaches. I expected that jacks and barracuda would be the main sport fish and indeed they were, but there were also some surprises!

It was on one of the rocky flats that I saw the biggest shoal of permit, including the biggest permit I have ever seen, and I watched a dozen or so of these massive permit feeding for quite a length of time. They were moving powerfully in water about 3 feet deep, and every so often one would upend and expose the thick wrist of a huge tail. Even if I had had my rod with me I couldn't have fished for them as they were too far offshore and I still wonder how big those permit were.

My first sighting of bonefish came a couple of days later when Sue and I were sightseeing in a small settlement called Leverick Bay. The settlement had a beach and dock and I spotted what I thought was a small shark moving next to the dock, but on closer inspection it turned out to be a bonefish. I am not going to estimate the weight, but the fact that my first thought was that the fish was a shark should give an idea of how big the bonefish was and, to this day, it still is the largest I have seen.

After that encounter I kept an eye out for more bonefish and, whilst out kayaking one morning close to my hotel, I saw a small shoal that were feeding over an area of rocky flat. It was this sighting that made me determined to catch some.

The next sighting was, bizarrely, whilst I was having breakfast the following morning. Sue and I were staying at the Biras Creek hotel. The restaurant was on the first floor and looked out over a boat dock which was situated in a picturesque bay surrounded by mangroves. The dock was in deep water so that boats could get in and out, but beyond this was a shallow area of soft, brown marl that stretched out to the mangroves. Eating breakfast and

Splendid isolation.

My first big bonefish from Long Island.

Trevor wondering where all the bonefish have gone.

They are out there somewhere!

looking out on what was a very pleasant view, I suddenly noticed three big bonefish appear out of the deep water and swim across the shallow marl towards the mangroves – so there were bonefish around that I could fish for!

Later that morning I was standing on the dock looking for the bonefish and it wasn't long before I found them. They were about a 100 yards away and I could clearly see three good-sized fish patrolling up and down close to the mangroves. The difficult part was going to be getting into a position from where I could cast to them. It would be impossible to wade in the very soft marl to where they were, and from where I was standing the mangroves looked impenetrable. However, the mangrove route gave me the only possible chance of getting close to the bonefish and, however slim, it was my only option. So I made my way back along the landing stage and walked over to the area where the mangroves were.

When I reached the mangroves I found a small path running behind them which I walked up and down for a while, trying to find a way through. The mangroves were at about head height, which meant it wasn't possible to see much, and there was about 20 feet of what looked like very thick, impenetrable undergrowth. Not to be deterred, on closer inspection I found just one part of the mangrove that wasn't quite as thick as the rest and with a bit of twisting and manoeuvring I could just make my way through to the water's edge. I stood at the edge of the mangrove scanning the water for some time hoping that the bonefish would appear and sure enough the pod of three bonefish swam past, oblivious to my presence.

I must have watched them for quite some time whilst working out how to catch one. Because of where I was standing there was absolutely no way I was ever going to get in a back cast, but to my left there was a clear patch of sand, so I decided to flick my fly onto that hoping the bonefish would swim over it. I was reasonably confident that this would work as they had patrolled up and down the mangrove edge half a dozen times whilst I had been watching and each time they had passed over the lighter patch. So I waited until they had turned at the far end of their route and were once again heading my way before flicking out the fly.

I was finding this whole episode thoroughly enthralling as it was so different from my normal approach to bonefishing. The bonefish were now well on the way to the clear patch of sand and I only had to wait a few moments before they arrived at the chosen spot. Having watched them for what must have been 15 minutes as they patrolled up and down I knew they were on the lookout for food. It was clear to see they were actively foraging for any likely looking food item, so it was no surprise that all three bonefish hammered into the fly the second I moved it, but of course only one could take it. Having studied the three fish there was one at around 9 pounds, another maybe a pound smaller and the other a 5 pounder and it was the middle fish I found myself attached to.

Virgin Gorda

One often hears tales of how far a bonefish will run, although in reality I rarely had a fish run more than 100 yards, but this was one of the those occasions when the backing on the spool was going to be made to work. The bonefish took off at an incredible speed and just never stopped. I probably would have landed it if it hadn't have been for the dock, but the entrance to the small harbour area was about 150 yards away and I lost the bonefish as it swam out of the harbour and turned right!

I suppose I should have been disappointed at losing the fish, but I wasn't as I had just spent an absorbing time watching feeding bonefish at very close quarters, which were oblivious to my presence. What's more, I had done all the hard stuff and, precariously perched in amongst the mangroves, had managed to hook one of the bonefish. Landing one would have been just icing on the cake.

Throughout the remainder of my stay I never saw the bonefish in the dock again, although I continued to look for them. To my surprise I did find a small, genuine bonefish flat not more than a mile from the hotel. A more accurate description would be a pancake flat and getting there involved renting a small Boston Whaler. This gave me the chance to be my own guide for a while and catch some bonefish, although they weren't as big as the "shark" bonefish or those around the dock. The flat wasn't that big and the tide had to be just right before the bonefish appeared. It took me several trips to work out their movements, but this is all part of do-it-yourself bonefishing.

A Bonefishing Journey

The journey to the flat was across a large, deep bay and on one occasion I saw some very big tarpon. I didn't fish for them as I only had my bonefish gear with me, but it gives an indication of the fishing potential of the region. The tarpon were well in excess of 100 pounds and that, along with the sightings of the monster permit and my "shark" bonefish, suggests the area could deliver some surprise captures!

I haven't been back to Virgin Gorda since that time, but definitely plan to do so, as there certainly are some very big bonefish, permit and tarpon waiting to be caught. The fishing there is so different from my usual bonefishing which makes it all the more appealing. I believe there are now fishing guides working the area, but for the angler who enjoys fishing on his own the British Virgin Islands have a lot to offer. I'm sure that on my two trips to the island I have only managed to scratch the surface.

Chapter 6

Andros

Once the bonefish bug really takes hold then sooner or later Andros will come into view. It is easily the largest of the Bahamian islands being about 80 miles in length and 50 miles across at its widest point. It is also the epicentre for very serious bonefishing, certainly in the Bahamas, but equally so throughout the world, and much of the history and folklore that surrounds bonefishing is linked to Andros. It probably has more fishable bonefish flats than all of the other Bahamian islands put together, but there is also an astonishing diversity of bonefish habitat the like of which I haven't seen elsewhere in the Bahamas. It is for this reason that, despite numerous forays to other bonefish destinations, I will continue to return to Andros again and again.

The major pulling point is the sheer number of bonefish that inhabit Andros, plus the high average size of fish. It is not uncommon to catch a dozen fish in a day where the majority will be between 4 and 6 pounds and this can be done on a regular basis. There is also the chance of a genuine monster – some of the bonefish I have seen on the West Side have been well into double figures and 12- to 13-pound bonefish are caught from time to time.

The other important point that I have already alluded to is the diversity of habitat and for this reason I am using a separate chapter to cover the Joulter Cays region to the north of the island. This chapter will focus on the North Bight, the West Side and the East Side, all of which offer quite separate bonefishing experiences in their own right.

My first visit to Andros was with Trevor. We made the usual trip out from Heathrow via Nassau, finally arriving, after a very long travelling day, at the Andros Island Bonefish Club. The club, on Cargill Creek, is ideally situated to fish the East Side flats. What is more, it also gives easy access to the North Bight which cuts right through the centre of the island. The Bight is a huge expanse of flats and mangroves holding vast numbers of bonefish. Sometimes when the tides are high it is easy to think that the area is devoid of bonefish, but this is simply because they will have moved into the extensive mangrove areas to feed. However, there are times when the tides are, for whatever reason, just right and on such occasions there will be bonefish everywhere and the fishing seems too easy. If you continue through the North Bight you finally arrive on the West Side of the island which offers some of the very best bonefishing anywhere.

Fishing the North Bight is mostly over soft marl, which is oozy soft mud and really impossible to wade. I have tried to wade there on several occasions when the water was too shallow for the skiff to reach a big tailing bonefish, and despite some sage advice from my guide telling me that I would get stuck, I amply proved the point moments later! So the only sensible option for fishing the Bights is to fish from the skiff.

Although I had been bonefishing for several years, by the time I got round to fishing Andros, apart from a few days out with Docky Smith on Long Island, I had done very little fishing from a skiff and had spent most of the time wade fishing. On the one hand this was a good thing, as it gave me time to think about what I was doing and I was able to watch the bonefish at close quarters and understand and learn their behaviour. However, this relaxed style of bonefishing doesn't have the pressure of casting from a skiff to big, single fish in difficult casting conditions whilst being watched by your guide and boat partner, which is very much the norm on Andros. It took me a while to be able to forget about the spectators at the end of the boat and to be able to cast quickly and accurately to big bonefish in demanding weather conditions and under pressure – but I got there in the end.

Fishing the Bights is generally done close to the mangroves and guides will normally pole the boat to within 50 yards of the shoreline. The bonefish here, as on the West Side, seem to have a real sense of purpose and more often than not will be hugging the shoreline and travelling at speed against the tide. This means that the skiff, which is being carried with the tide, will meet, and pass, bonefish which are travelling quickly towards it. Sometimes it is all you can do to get a cast out quickly enough to be in with a chance of covering fish before they speed by. When the tides are running the bonefish travel in fairly large groups and it is not uncommon to have schools of 100 or more bonefish approaching, which is a great sight! When the tide lessens there will be further opportunities to go for singles or doubles that cruise just a few feet from the shore. This is where the guides really earn their money as they skilfully manoeuvre the skiff into the right position for the angler to get a good cast at the bonefish. Sometimes it is possible to follow a single fish maybe 100 yards or so and get off several casts before hooking up. When this happens it's a cause of great excitement in the boat as everyone is involved one way or another in the capture.

The fishing on the West Side is similar to the Bights in that the fish travel in groups, but that is where the similarities end. The West Side, as the name implies, runs down the west side of Andros and offers fantastic bonefish for much of its 80-mile length. The West Side is made up of long stretches of marl beaches interspersed with mangrove-lined creeks that the bonefish run up at high tide. To get to the West Side involves an hour-long ride in the skiff which, in windy conditions, is a battering experience and not for the faint hearted. In fact, it is not possible to effectively fish the West Side if there is even a moderate westerly, onshore wind, as it really churns the water into a milky state that makes fishing impossible. However, the rough ride is nearly always worth it.

Another strange weather related phenomenon that you need to be aware of is that the West Side is often not fishable after prolonged, heavy rain. The reason is that at low tide large, rain filled puddles will accumulate on the white marl shoreline. When the tide comes in the sea water mixes with the puddles of freshwater which results in large volumes of rusty coloured water lining the shore. This puts a complete stop to the fishing until the next cycle of the tide. I have been caught out a few times by this, so I normally give the West Side a miss if there has been very heavy overnight rain.

The exit from the North Bight on to the West Side is always exciting as it is through a deep channel that emerges onto a massive flat that stretches to the horizon and on a still, cloudless day it is difficult to distinguish where the sea ends and the sky begins. This is yet another example of why fishing a bonefish flat can be so very special. Once through the entrance and following a sharp right turn the fishing begins and you can expect, when the tide is right, to have consistent shots at bonefish schools as they move at speed against the tide hugging the shoreline. For some reason these schools always seem to come at about 15-minute intervals and always travel in a southerly direction. Maybe they do go in the opposite direction, but I have never seen this and the view held by the guides is that they travel round the whole island. However, I don't subscribe to this view as you would see similar behaviour on the East Side and Joulter Cays but it doesn't happen there. I suspect that this behaviour will have to remain an unsolved Andros mystery but it's nice not to know everything and to have a few mysteries to ponder back at the lodge over dinner.

When the fish are running it is possible to fish from a stationary boat tied to a push pole just a few feet from the shore. The bonefish tightly hug the contours of the shore and many of the schools are so big it is possible to see them 400 yards away or, if is cloudy, the nervous water they produce. This can be very exciting as the large schools approach at speed and the real challenge is getting the timing and positioning of the cast just right; cast too early and the fly may rest on the bottom but be in the wrong place, cast too late and the fly may still be sinking as the bonefish pass underneath it. So the ideal is to cast just ahead of the fast moving shoal, so that the fly has enough time to reach the bottom, which allows you to start the retrieve just when the bonefish are moving over it. Sometimes the larger fish will be in the centre or rear of the school, so it pays to let a few of the smaller bonefish pass over the fly before the retrieve is started. Quite often I have caught bigger than average-sized bonefish as a result of this tactic.

I have found the choice of fly to be critical on Andros and the pattern, weight and size all need to be just right. If it isn't then catches will suffer. When I first fished Andros

I felt I had a pretty good idea of which flies would work, but this soon came under scrutiny just a few days into my first trip. My flies where often ignored and I was left with the impression that the fish either weren't interested in them or they weren't even seen by the bonefish. When I discussed this with the guides it soon became apparent that the flies that regularly caught bonefish on Andros were completely different to those that were available from the fly fishing outlets.

The fly of choice in Andros is the Gotcha. This is not surprising as it first came into being on the island, but as I have already intimated the Andros Gotcha bears little resemblance to its shop-bought cousin. Firstly, it is much bigger and is often tied on a size 2 hook. It is also necessary to fish it with lead eyes so that it quickly reaches the bottom and becomes attractive to fast moving bonefish in deepish water. And, finally, it needs to be bushy with a substantial craft fur wing that means the fly can be 2 to 3 inches in length.

I well remember when Trevor and I were being guided by Rupert Leadon, who is credited with naming the Gotcha, and as he said that day, "Your fly needs plenty of allure!" which is what these big Gotchas have. There is no way that an Andros-sized Gotcha is not going to be seen by the bonefish! This last point is especially important on the West Side as the average depth of water is deeper than perhaps you would experience on most flats, so the fly has to get down to the bonefish and be seen. The West

Side bonefish really do like these big Gotchas and when they are in a feeding mood will jump on the fly.

With such great fishing available on the West Side and through the Bights, the fishing on the East Side somehow gets forgotten on Andros, which is a pity as it can offer bonefishing of the very highest order. The fishing there is mostly over hard, white sand which means that, unlike the North Bight and the West Side, the East Side gives the opportunity of some excellent wade fishing. The bonefish there are of a specimen size that is comparable to the rest of Andros. I well remember hooking two very big bonefish one morning that were well into double figures, only to lose both as they disappeared at speed into the mangroves. What makes the East Side fishing so difficult for much of the time is the prevailing easterly wind. This often renders the fishing impossible, but on days when the wind drops the fishing can be superb. I have found that the guides seem to overlook the East Side, even when the weather is perfect, so it is well worth asking your guide to give the East Side a try if the conditions look ideal.

All of my fishing around the North Bight, West Side and East Side has been out of the Andros Island Bonefish Club and the lodge, as I have mentioned, is ideally situated on Cargill Creek, which gives good access to all three of these areas. The lodge, like so many of the fishing lodges on Andros, has very experienced and professional guides, which reflects the island's long heritage as a premier bonefish destination.

Andros

All my bonefish trips have produced memorable experiences and I have many from Andros, but the one that particularly sticks in my mind was when Trevor and I had spent a day fishing with David Neymour as our guide. We always enjoyed fishing with David because he is a first-class guide and great company. On this particular day he had done his best to put us on fish, but by early afternoon we had just a couple of bonefish each for our efforts. The morning had been spent fishing the West Side, but it was unusually quiet so we had moved back in to the North Bight and were fishing an area known as the Dressing Room. We had stopped for a late lunch and the boat was moored up to the pole at the point of a very large bay. From our position we could clearly see the other point of the bay way off in the distance.

Just as we were thinking about our strategy for the afternoon something just changed. The light became less bright as a bank of faint clouds suddenly appeared and enveloped the island, and the wind got up just enough to create that sudden fishing feeling that you cannot put your finger on but know is there. We sat for maybe 5 minutes discussing this when David said, "Quick, one of you, get your rod, there's some fish coming."

It was Trevor's turn to fish from the front of the boat, and whilst he was getting ready as quickly as he could I was looking out to see where the bonefish were, but I couldn't see a thing. I scanned the water up to 200 yards from the boat, but I couldn't see any fish there so I asked

David where the fish were and he told me to look to the other point of the bay. The point must have been 600 yards away and sure enough there was the biggest area of nervous water I had ever seen – and it was moving straight across the bay directly towards us!

Because the bay was so large we waited in eager anticipation, but amazingly when the huge push of nervous water was about half way across the bay another equally large push of bonefish rounded the far-off point. So we had two huge groups of bonefish heading for us and, not surprisingly, I got my rod ready too. When the first group arrived there were so many bonefish, and they were travelling so quickly, that it was possible to hear the push of water. Trevor cast his fly just ahead of the nervous water and had to strip the fly really fast to make a hook up which he did. It is always worth remembering that when there is a push of nervous water, the fish aren't directly under the disturbed water but are actually under the smooth area that precedes it, so it is important to cast well ahead of the push and start stripping straight away. I also use large bead chain eyes, or even lead eyes, to make sure that the fly sinks as quickly as possible.

Once Trevor had hooked his fish there was just enough time for me to get up to the front of the boat and get off a cast to the next shoal, and sure enough we were soon both into fish. What we hadn't noticed was that while we were concentrating on the first two pushes, another had appeared around the far off point and then, just a few minutes later, it was followed by yet another. This chain of events continued throughout the remainder of the afternoon until, finally, it became just too dark to see, but even then we could still hear the bonefish continuing their efforts to push their way across the bay.

I can't remember exactly how many bonefish we caught that afternoon, but it was a lot and it was easily the best day's bonefishing Trevor and I had ever had. This wasn't just because we caught a large number of bonefish, or because they were of a high average size, but that the fishing was so exhilarating and visual. What was so special was that this was Andros giving a demonstration of why it is such an outstanding place to go bonefishing.

Like many of the Bahamian islands I wouldn't describe Andros as a mixed fishery; it is predominantly a bonefish island, but there are other species to be caught and I have certainly seen some good tarpon swimming around. I usually plan my trips for November, which I consider the best time for catching large numbers of better than average-sized bonefish, but this is not the best time for permit and tarpon. I am sure there are more of them around earlier in the year, in May or June.

There is an abundance of barracuda and sharks and for the angler who targets them, there is good sport to be had. In fact, I have never fished anywhere that has quite so many sharks as Andros; they are a permanent feature on any bonefish flat which can be a real hindrance when trying to land a bonefish. The guides on Andros have a variety of tactics they employ to keep them away and Elias, who guides in the north of the island, has a three-pronged spear that he will hurl at any shark that comes close, although I have never seen him hit one! This is quite effective for scaring sharks in the north of Andros where the hard flats makes chasing sharks a possibility, but is more difficult in the Bights and West Side as you are confined to the boat for most of the time as the depth and soft marl makes wading difficult. Because of this the sharks have it all their own way and can come right up to the boat and very easily chomp a bonefish in half. The only tactic that can be employed here is to try and bully a hooked bonefish and wind like crazy but, of course, this is easier said than done! I have found on Andros that it pays to be philosophical about the sharks and accept that over a week's fishing they will inevitably take a few bonefish.

Of course, the plus side of sharks is that you can fish for them and I have experienced a few tussles with them myself and seen some good captures. The best of them all was when Phil caught a 100 pound shark while we were drinking cocktails in the open-air bar of the Andros Island Bonefish Club.

The usual routine after a day's fishing on Andros is to arrive back at the lodge in the late afternoon, get showered and changed and then head to the bar for a drink or two before dinner. In the bar area there is a table with a hole in the middle, presumably were a parasol once stood, but there is now no umbrella, just the hole. Phil, who has

Andros

always approached fishing with a fair degree of lateral thinking, abandoned his beer, disappeared for a while and then returned with a boat rod and multiplier kitted out for shark fishing. He baited a very large hook with some barracuda that had been caught the day before and lowered it into Cargill Creek, which is just the other side of a small wall that surrounds the bar. Finally, he placed the rod in the hole in the centre of the table and calmly resumed drinking his beer.

The other anglers in the group found this highly amusing and there was a brief discussion about the chances of catching a shark, but after a while the topic changed, the conversation moved on and we all forgot about the shark rod. The table was about 6 feet from the wall, the rod was in its hole, pointing at the sky and the line was in a gentle curve from the rod tip to the wall before going over the side into the creek. Along the top of the wall were some small, black ornamental lights and as there was a gentle breeze Phil's line had come to rest under one of them.

The murmur of conversation had gradually grown louder as more Kaliks were consumed, and we were all starting to remark that dinner wouldn't be long when suddenly Phil's table started to shudder its way across the bar patio towards the small wall. The rod was arched over and the line, which was now under considerable tension, went straight down to one of the small ornamental lamps on the wall. This meant a shark was one side of the lamp and the heavy table was on the other. The poor little lamp didn't stand a chance, it was suddenly catapulted high into the air and at exactly the same time a huge cheer went up from the crowd in the bar! At precisely the same moment Phil was running to save his rod from being dragged into the water, he only just made it and was soon attached to what was clearly a decent shark.

There is nothing better than having a large gathering of anglers, who have enjoyed a few drinks, watching another angler play a big fish and it was fair to say that Phil wasn't short of advice. Not surprisingly, dinner had to be delayed as we watched for what seemed an age before Phil finally beached his shark on the slipway next to the bar. What followed was a very memorable evening as Phil relived the epic battle over dinner and the tale became longer and more dramatic with each Kalik – but it was certainly a great evening for all concerned.

As I have already said there are also plenty of barracuda on Andros and I have taken them to nearly 20 pounds, but pride of place goes to my friend Vincent who had one that was simply huge. He also caught the barracuda on a fly, which takes some doing, and he landed it despite having his rod smashed in the process. He was out fishing with Rambo, who is one of the guides at the Bonefish Club and, as his name suggests, he isn't a small bloke. The photo of Rambo groaning as he holds up the barracuda just shows how big the fish was, it must have been 40 pounds – a truly superb fish.

Looking through my fishing diary I have had three trips

Andros

to the Andros Island Bonefish Club and have had excellent fishing on each occasion, with good numbers of bonefish and a high average weight. As far as bonefish destinations go, the middle part of Andros is a superb area of diverse habitat that offers a genuine chance of a double-digit bonefish. It isn't as commercialized or built-up as some of the other islands and bonefishing is regarded as a main source of income on the island and treated with respect. Andros is certainly a destination that any serious bonefisher should visit at some stage.

Chapter 7

Harbour Island

Most of my bonefish trips are the result of extensive research followed by careful planning with fishing friends, but my first trip to Harbour Island was determined, most emphatically, by my wife Sue. The year before we had been on a week's holiday to Eleuthera during which I had managed to mix in a few bonefishing sessions with sightseeing on the island. One of the sightseeing jaunts was to Harbour Island which lies at the northern tip of Eleuthera and is a short 10-minute water taxi ride away.

I was fully aware of Harbour Island as a bonefishing destination and, as anyone who has read Dick Brown's excellent and very informative book on bonefishing will know, much of what he wrote about bonefishing takes place on the island. Dick's book, however, wasn't unique in featuring Harbour Island, it was also central to Stanley M. Babson's *Bonefishing*, which was probably the first book dedicated solely to the sport. If you are lucky enough to get hold of a copy of Babson's book you will be treated to some superb black and white photos of him fishing with the legendary guide, Bonefish Joe. For such a small island tucked away in the Bahamas, Harbour Island has played an important role in furthering the sport and techniques of bonefishing.

What surprised me, following that short water taxi ride, is how different Harbour Island was to elsewhere I had visited in the Bahamas – Sue and I were greeted by a captivating scene that is more reminiscent of Martha's Vineyard. Harbour Island, though a busy, built-up place is nevertheless, delightful. The island is not large, it is about 3 miles long and one side has the most spectacular beach of soft pink sand that is constantly photographed and often appears in glossy travel magazines. Many of the houses are of clapperboard construction, hence the similarity with Martha's Vineyard, and are painted in a variety of pastel colours. As there are very few cars on the island, the transport of choice is the golf cart; on our first visit Sue and I spent most of the time exploring the island in one, only interrupting the journey to stop at one of the excellent hotels to grab a brochure and drink a cold Kalik!

By the time we boarded the water taxi it was late in the afternoon and Sue had decided that we most certainly should return the following year, but for a whole week. Of course, I was perfectly happy with this suggestion as it would give me another chance at some bonefishing and, sure enough, the following May we were back. We were staying at The Landing, a delightful small boutique hotel which looks out over the harbour. Each morning breakfast is served on a ground level veranda, an ideal vantage point to soak up the mood of the island and watch the world go by. In fact it was possible, if the tide was right, to eat breakfast and watch tailing bonefish in the harbour, which was always a nice start to the day!

Whenever I go fishing with fellow bonefishers it is always full-on fishing every day, but when Sue and I are on holiday I know there has to be some balance. As much as I would like to fish daily, I knew I was probably only going to get a away with a couple of days bonefishing and that it would not be prudent to start bonefishing too soon into the holiday.

On our first morning we were just settling into our breakfast when Sue spotted this very tall, cigar smoking man walking along the road towards us. He was carrying a fly rod and was decked out in the usual bonefish uniform and, as a good spotter of bonefishers, she pointed him out. He also noticed us, so crossed the small road and came over for a chat.

Jack was an American from Maine and, as you do, we immediately started talking about bonefishing. I am always amazed at how angling brings perfect strangers together who, within minutes, become the best of friends. Jack was a larger-than-life character with a great sense of humour and I was soon invited to share a guide and boat with him the following day – of course I had to accept. I remember Jack's invitation, "If you can put up with me all day and I can put up with you, then I'll buy you a beer at the end of it." I had no doubt that we would be enjoying a beer late the following afternoon!

The next day dawned and after meeting up, Jack and I slowly made our way to the dock. By the time we arrived there it was obvious to me that "putting up with Jack" would be no chore at all as he was already delightful and amusing company. We also had an excellent guide in Patrick Roberts, who was everything a good guide should be in that he was very enjoyable company and was first class when it came to spotting fish, especially when it was cloudy and windy.

The fishing on Harbour Island was a real surprise to me and was nothing like nearby Eleuthera. I didn't have high expectations as far as the fishing was concerned, but to the west of Harbour Island was large area of fishable flats and creeks, a habitat that was very reminiscent of the Bights area on Andros. I also discovered that the bonefish, on average, were bigger than those on Eleuthera, so all in all it is a very fine destination and I can fully understand why it figures so prominently in Dick Brown's book.

Our day with Patrick proved to be both enjoyable and productive and Jack and I caught plenty of bonefish. Some were taken whilst wading the surprisingly large flats and the others were caught poling from the skiff in the creeks and the deeper shoreline. Not surprisingly, after such a good time, Jack and I thoroughly enjoyed our beers in the hotel at the end of the day!

I fished with Jack a couple more times during that week on Eleuthera. In addition to the Bight-like area to the west of Harbour Island there is some excellent wade fishing over very hard, white sand on what is known as the Girls Flat, and Jack and I would fish here when the tide was right. Having fished all over the Bahamas and Caribbean, I am of the view that the Girls Flat bonefish are the most intelligent and difficult to catch. On that first visit to Harbour Island, I remember fishing the flat on a number of occasions and being surrounded by tailing bonefish, but finding it almost impossible to catch them. I did eventually have some success, but only after I started using 14-foot leaders with a size 8 fly. They were also very picky about what pattern they would take and a small orange crab option seemed to out-fish everything else. The other thing that was crucial to catching these bonefish was that the fly needed to be totally stationary and the normal strip strip retrieve would spook the fish every time. Despite never really catching bonefish in numbers from the Girls Flat I found the fishing totally absorbing. It was a reminder that bonefish can at times prove to be a very smart adversary and difficult to catch.

The other time I fished with Jack was when we decided to do some do-it-yourself boat fishing for bonefish. Something that is quite unusual at Harbour Island is that you can hire a Boston Whaler which gives the bonefisher the chance to access some of the large flats areas just a short boat ride to the north of Harbour Island. We decided not to attempt to fish the Bights area, as this would need considerable knowledge of tides and depths, and instead headed for the Man Island flats just to the north of Harbour Island. This was considered a fairly straightforward affair which would involve mooring the boat on a beach and then fishing the flat – or so we thought!

We collected the boat from the dock and made our way to Man Island. Sure enough, the white sandy beach was exactly as we expected so we motored up to it and eased the boat on to the sandy beach. The tide was about to start coming in, which would be ideal for bonefishing, so we tossed the anchor high up on to the beach and eagerly made our way to the large expanse of hard, white sand flat that was just a short walk away. By now it was late morning so the flat had had plenty of time to warm up and would be a good temperature for the bonefish as the tide started to cover it.

For the next hour or so Jack and I were totally engrossed in the bonefishing. There were plenty of bonefish about but, as with the Girls Flat, they were very spooky and clever and we remained fishless. I was, nevertheless, confident that it would only be a matter of time until one of them picked up my small crab pattern.

I'm sure that we would have caught some bonefish, but just as I was getting into the fishing I glanced up and saw a boat exactly the same as ours about 100 yards offshore. In fact it was our boat, but how could that be? I looked up the beach and there was the anchor and its rope still lying on the sand! Of course, we should have checked when we got on board, but you sort of expect anchors to be tied to boats.

The immediate problem was how to get the boat, which was now drifting steadily into ever deeper water. As we didn't have much time, I started to wade as fast as I could towards the boat but, with 30 yards still to go, I was up to my chest in water – there was no way I was going to reach it. As luck would have it, another boat saw us and towed the boat and me to the shore, so in the end everything turned out OK. By the time we had reorganized ourselves the flat was too deep to fish, so we called it a day, licking our wounds and vowing to check the boat more thoroughly next time!

Apart from the boating incident, that first week on Harbour Island was immensely enjoyable, it had that rare combination of a first-class holiday destination coupled with some quality bonefishing. Not surprisingly, Sue and I were back again the following year, this time at the Coral Sands hotel – another excellent place to stay – which looked out over the pink sands of the beach. Without my newly found bonefishing buddy Jack, I was fishing on my own most of the time, but Sue did accompany me to the Girls Flat a couple of times where she became adept at spotting bonefish and, on another occasion, she joined me on the skiff with Robert.

Harbour Island

It was during a day fishing with Robert that we had a salutary reminder of the vagaries of the Bahamian weather, the importance of having waterproof clothing and a very experienced guide. The day had started just fine and after being collected from the dock by Robert we motored across the bay to the mangroves and flats on the other side. The weather was perfect, with clear blue skies and a gentle breeze. Halfway through the first drift we found some bonefish and I kicked off the day with a nice 5 pounder; the omens looked good!

For the next hour or so I continued to catch whilst Sue busied herself taking photos and spotting turtles which, on that particular day, kept popping up all over the place. By lunchtime the clouds had started to suddenly build and at about the same time Robert and I spotted a big bone tailing about a 100 yards or so away, so we left the boat and waded off in hot pursuit. The tailer was continually moving and as the bottom was a mixture of hard sand and marl we struggled to keep up, and although I did manage to get in a couple of casts we soon lost sight of the fish. By this time we must have been 400 yards from the skiff and it was then that we noticed two very large, ominous black cloud formations: one to the west of the island and one to the east. We weren't unduly concerned at that point because the weather immediately above us was fine, but the wind had suddenly sprung up and we assumed that the two ominous cloud systems would probably go their separate ways. Oh, how wrong we were!

A Bonefishing Journey

By the time we were back at the skiff it was clear that the cloud systems were rapidly moving together on a collision course, and Robert had only one thing on his mind which was to head for home as quickly as possible. The ride back to the Harbour Island dock should have taken about 15 minutes, but we were only 5 minutes into the journey when the two cloud systems clattered into each other and all hell broke loose. Day became night and rain literally fell out of the sky as the wind whipped itself up into a fury and lightening crashed all around us. Not surprisingly, I had seen this coming and both Sue and I had put on our waterproof wading jackets with the hoods up and firmly tide down; all we could do was to keep our heads down and away from the relentless and by now very cold rain. It is at times like this that your guide takes the brunt of the storm as they have to continue to drive back, but by now the weather was so awful that visibility was no more than 20 yards and there was no way that Robert could navigate the skiff as there was nowhere in sight to navigate to. A Plan B was urgently needed and, as if by magic, Robert found us a cave! I was amazed that there was a cave on the island and even more surprised that Robert had found it in such a diabolical storm, but it meant that we were out of the relentless rain and wind. Sheltering in the cave gave us an opportunity to take stock and regain some composure.

We must have been in the cave for about an hour and the plan was to stay there until the storm abated, but this was not happening. The storm just continued on and on and in the end we had no option but to try and make it home. The visibility was still almost non existent but, despite that, Robert miraculously got us safely back to the dock and to this day I don't know how he managed it. The storm actually continued well into late afternoon and, as so often happens in the Bahamas, by early evening Sue and I were sipping cocktails by the pool and the weather was perfect again. *C'est la vie!*

I had one more trip out with Robert later that week. The tides were just right, and so was the weather, and we spent a very pleasant day poling across the flats catching some nice bones. At times like this it is hard to imagine that bonefishing can be anything other than perfect, but the experience we had just a couple of days beforehand should always be a reminder that when out on the flats you should always have adequate protective clothing.

Harbour Island is a wonderful place to visit and it is unusual to experience such good bonefishing whilst at the same time having the opportunity to stay at high quality hotels and dine in fine restaurants. I find the fishing there interesting due to the diversity of habitat and there is always the chance of catching one of the very big bonefish which are undoubtedly there. I am sure that it will only be a matter of time before Sue and I are there again!

Chapter 8

Joulter Cays

Trevor and I first met David and Gordon in Havana, on our way out to Cayo Largo for a week's fishing. All four of us had paid an extra fifty quid to get VIP check-in at the José Martí International Airport in Havana which, as the queues are so long, is highly recommended and well worth the extra money. Part of the deal is that you are whizzed through immigration and then taken to a smart lounge with very comfortable leather sofas and then plied with cold beer, so it is no great hardship. During this time, your bags are tracked down, which can take at least an hour and often more, giving ample time to relax and talk with fellow bonefishers who are on the flight. On this particular occasion Trevor and I started a conversation with David and Gordon and it soon became clear that we all had similar bonefishing experiences and, perhaps more importantly, the same sense of humour.

That first meeting cemented our friendships and several years later, having had a couple more trips to Cuba, all four of us were now on our way to Andros to fish Joulter Cays,

Joulter Cays

which is at the northern tip of the island. What's so convenient about the Bahamas is that from the UK you can get to your fishing destination on the same day, but the timing can be a little tight. The Heathrow flight lands in Nassau mid-afternoon which leaves just about an hour to catch the connecting flight to your chosen out island. To be fair, I have always managed this, but on a couple of occasions it has been a very close call and far too stressful, which is not the ideal start to a week's bonefishing! However, this time, as there were four of us, it was actually cheaper to get our own private pilot and plane for the second leg of the journey. This meant we didn't have to wait for the normal scheduled departure, but simply take a taxi to the nearby general aviation terminal, meet up with our pilot and be on our way. And this is exactly what happened. I always enjoy these trips in a small plane as it often gives a wonderful view of the flats you are likely to be fishing. The flight out to Andros takes maybe half an hour at most and on this trip it was clear and sunny. It gave us all a wonderful view of the Joulter Cays area and the East Side flats as we approached North Andros airport.

The main reason behind this trip was to catch some bonefish wading. Unlike the Middle Bights further south and the West Side where the fishing is, for the most part, from a skiff over a soft marl bottom, Joulter Cays offers superb wade fishing. We were staying with Phillip Rolle and Betsy Sandstrom-Rolle in Nicholls Town, where they run a first-class operation with most of their fishing taking place in the north of Andros. The four of us would fish from two skiffs with Elias as our second guide.

The Joulter Cays area covers perhaps 150 square miles and is yet another example of the beauty and diversity of habitat that bonefishing exposes the angler to. The wade fishing here is as good as it gets and although I have seen larger areas of flats, I have never seen flats that give as much continuous wading as Joulters. If the tide is right, it is possible to park up the skiff and just keep wading for as long as you want! Not only is the area vast but it is, for the most part, easy and pleasant wading unlike many flats where there are pockets of marl that unexpectedly suck you in to thigh-deep goo. Joulters is virtually all hard, white sand where you can comfortably wade and concentrate on the fishing at the same time.

My first visit to Joulters was mid-November and Trevor and I were out with Phillip on the first day. I like bonefishing trips in November as the fish certainly like to shoal up at that time of year and the average size seems to be better than in May, which is the other time I favour. The weather in November can be very good with water temperatures on the flats well into the 70s, which is ideal for bonefish. Even when the temperature drops a few degrees there is still the chance of finding larger fish in ones and twos. However, the downside with this time of year is that cold fronts can come down from the north and, as the name suggests, they can be very cold. And on this particular day the bonefishing was as cold as I can ever remember. I can

Joulter Cays

picture quite vividly the sharp shock as I stepped over the side of the skiff into what felt like ice water; any optimism I had quickly dropped along with the temperature. In addition to the cold water there was a stiff, biting wind and the clouds were thick and grey, so all in all it wasn't the most perfect weather for bonefishing.

Despite the conditions, Trevor and I, encouraged by Phillip, started to talk the day up: of course it would be warmer later, maybe the wind would drop and the sun would shine! We wandered across the flat for what seemed an age but saw nothing, not even a shark or ray which is never a good sign as when they are about so, generally, are the bonefish! The flat was a dull grey that mirrored the sky but we continued on for some time and were fairly close to the end of the wade when, as if by magic, there in front of me were half a dozen bonefish. As often happens on these windy cloudy days, they were so easy to see and appeared almost black against the apparent greyness of the sand. It's a strange paradox that at the end of a week's bonefishing I can put the fly, whatever the conditions, in exactly the right spot, but on the first day of a week's fishing I am always a little rusty and sure enough I fluffed that first cast. I always find this embarrassing, especially with a guide who I haven't fished with before, as I sense them looking on wondering if they are in for a hard week!

The great thing about bonefishing is that when you do get the cast wrong you generally get another chance fairly soon and, sure enough, almost moments later along came

A Bonefishing Journey

another pod of black-looking bonefish. This time I made no mistake and had my first fish of the week. I was up and running and Phillip was smiling!

Despite my early concerns, that first day turned out to be really good and although the conditions were awful Trevor and I each had six good-sized bonefish. The fish became increasingly hungry as the day wore on and the temperature increased and, although they were picky about the fly in the morning, they would readily leap on the Gotcha in the afternoon. On returning to the dock that evening we discovered that both David and Gordon also had a similar catch. What looked as if it would be a tough day, turned into a fine start to the week's fishing.

The following day was one of those very special days on the flats that come along every so often and need to be appreciated and remembered. The cold front that had been so evident the previous day had disappeared and had been replaced by blue skies. The strong wind had also gone and we now had a perfect bonefishing wind which meant it wasn't too strong to make casting difficult, nor was it too gentle or calm, which can make bonefish nervous. We had agreed with David and Gordon that we should alternate guides, so today Trevor and I were fishing with Elias who, like Phillip, was very knowledge about fishing the Joulter Cays area as he had lived in the north of Andros all his life.

As I have mentioned before, the ride in a skiff is, on a good day, worth the day rate alone, and this day fell into that category. The Joulters are stunningly beautiful, especially when the sun is shining, and it was a pleasure just to soak up the scenery as we weaved our way between shallow sand flats and mangrove islands towards some place known only to Elias. The flats had lost the dull grey colour of the previous day and were now the most vivid white, which was in stark contrast to the deep blue of the sky. Eventually, after 20 minutes or so of soaking up each flat we zoomed past, the outboard started to ease off and we pulled up next to a small sandbar and gazed out on a wonderful, clean flat that continued to the horizon.

At times like this it is easy to be impatient and succumb to the temptation to get going straight away, but it is always worth just standing for a few minutes to take stock of the flat and to get everything ready, which is what Trevor and I did. Standing on the small sandbar we could see that the water over the flat was around a foot deep, so it would be unlikely that there would be any tailing fish until the tide went out later in the day. With a foot of water over the flat, the bonefish were likely to be shoaled up in one or two big groups. Sure enough, after scanning the flat from our sandbar eyrie we spotted a massive school of bonefish maybe 400 yards away, so we stepped into the nicely warm water that covered the flat – what a difference 24 hours can make!

What often happens with these large schools in shallow water is that they seem to graze their way across a flat at a speed that is just about wading pace. The bonefish appear to circulate in the school, so that the fish at the front are continually replaced by fish coming up from the centre of the school. Trevor and I positioned ourselves at either side of the bonefish, but the school seemed to work as one body and somehow managed to remain a very long cast away from both of us. Only about one in three casts would land far enough into the school of bonefish to give a genuine chance of a fish. We must have followed the bonefish for well over an hour, covering perhaps a mile, and it was fascinating to watch the constantly revolving school as it moved and grazed its way across the flat. Eventually, we had to stop because the bonefish found some deep water where it was impossible to wade, but we had each caught about seven good-sized fish, so it had been a great start to the day and it was still only late morning.

Joulter Cays has fabulous wade fishing and it is always possible to find one flat that has just the right amount of depth and this is often the case when the tide is falling for most of the fishing day. On this particular day, not only was the weather perfect, but so were the tides, and I knew that during the afternoon there would be an opportunity to fish for some tailing bonefish. It would have been easy to head off to another flat straight after our very productive morning session, but I always like to stop for lunch as it gives the chance to collect ones thoughts and maybe tie on a new leader or fly. Just as importantly, it gives your guide a well-earned rest, so we waded back to the sandbar for lunch and to discuss the tactics for the afternoon.

Joulter Cays

Our next port of call was a vast flat composed mostly of turtle grass at a depth which was just perfect for tailers. This was clearly evident by the number of glistening, waving bonefish tails on view. In fact, there were so many tailing fish that I knew I was going to be spoilt for choice over which fish to target first, but that wasn't going to be much of a hardship. My usual fly of choice when fishing for tailers over turtle grass is a crab type pattern, as the flats are stuffed full of them. The actual pattern isn't too critical, as long as it resembles a crab. I often use a Bonefish Bitters in orange which works well for me although I have also done well with a Borski Shrimp. What is important is that whatever fly you use it must have a weed guard, because without one the fly continually catches the weed and spooks the bonefish.

Fishing for tailing fish is, for me, the most pleasurable way to catch bonefish. It gives the angler the opportunity to fish alone and I often find myself so absorbed by the fishing that eventually, when I look up, I am a very long way from the skiff. It also brings out all the skills needed by the bonefisher, as it requires watercraft, stealth and the ability to deftly place the fly in exactly the right spot. On this particular afternoon the sun was in such a position that it made the bonefish tails stand out very prominently and they glistened like little mirrors betraying their presence. It was fascinating to watch big, single fish or pods of two or three, slowly work their way across the flat before suddenly plunging on something edible.

Over the years I have discovered that there are two strategies that work successfully on tailers. The first option is to cast about 3 feet in front of where you think the bonefish is heading and hope it continues on the same path. A cast any closer is likely to spook the fish and one further away means that the chances of the bonefish continuing ahead in the same direction and finding the fly are reduced. The second strategy, and it calls for fast, accurate casting, is to cast right on top of an upended bonefish when it has found something that takes its fancy. If you can put the fly as near to the head end as you can get, that's even better. They make so much commotion when they are actively searching out a prey item, they are completely unaware of the fly hitting the water. Providing the fly is in the right spot the bonefish will often be very aggressive when they take the fly.

During the afternoon Trevor and I just waded and waded across what seemed a never-ending flat, picking off bonefish as they came towards us – we must have had at least another dozen fish between us. The size of fish, as in the morning, was of a very high average with all the fish between 4 and 7 pounds. The bigger fish, of around the 6- and 7-pound mark, are immensely strong and catching tailing fish of this size is a truly spectacular event to witness, and be part of, as they charge through water that is barely covering their backs. Not surprisingly, this was a very special day for both of us and although on other occasions we have caught many more fish in a single day, the wonderful weather, the size of fish and the way that they were caught all combined to make this the perfect bonefishing experience.

That first visit to Joulter Cays was very memorable and all four of us had some great fishing as we explored the different flats and creeks. What also pleased me was that Joulters was every bit as good as I had hoped it would be and, as a wade fishing destination, it is superb. Not surprisingly, David, Gordon, Trevor and I were back again the following year when the fishing was even better as we used the knowledge we had gained from the first trip. We also had the previous experience of fishing with our excellent guides, Phillip and Elias, which also helps.

As with the first trip, we focused mainly on fishing for bonefish in the Joulters area but we also had a couple of excursions after permit. The first was to the very northern tip of the Joulter Cays, where the flats are a little deeper and therefore more suited to permit. The other outing was to Williams Island on the West Side of Andros. This involved taking the skiffs by trailer from the east coast of the island to the West Side and then making the very long trip in the skiff from there to Williams Island.

On both forays we didn't catch or see a permit, which is nothing unusual for me. Phillip explained that they are either around or not but, if they are, can be seen in good numbers. I would certainly like to have another go for them in May and June when they are more likely to be there than in November.

A Bonefishing Journey

The trip to the West Side proved interesting for several reasons. The journey there was pretty entertaining as we trailered both the skiffs over a fairly lengthy distance on rough roads and tracks. Once we had launched the boats it was still an hour's ride at full throttle in the skiff to Williams Islands so the journey was time consuming. For all the effort we were putting in I had hoped that it would be worth it, but in the end it turned out to be the worst day of the week for a couple of reasons. Although the day started off in bright sunshine and little in the way of wind, the weather soon became atrocious. The wind really got up and it rained very heavily and, to make matters worse, Phillip's skiff broke down on the return journey, so Elias had to tow it back which took forever.

If you go bonefishing often enough then sooner or later a day like this will come along and although they are frustrating, and sometimes uncomfortable, it pays to be philosophical. With luck, the following day is most likely to be warm and sunny and the trials and tribulations of the previous day will soon be a distant memory.

On the day at Williams Island one odd thing did happen which I have never seen or experienced before. Although for most of the time the weather was bad, we did have an hour or so of very still, warm weather before the storm arrived, which gave me the opportunity to do some meaningful fishing. I was up front and spotted a single, very big bonefish working its way close to the shore. Elias had seen it too, so he manoeuvred the skiff so that I could get a cast in, which I did placing my size 2 Andros Gotcha slightly ahead of the fish, then waited until the bonefish was close enough to see it. Once the fly was moved the bonefish nailed it, but instead of charging off, it just swam around close to the boat for a minute or so and then the hook pulled out.

I wasn't too happy about this as it was a big bonefish and I stood there for a while composing my thoughts and rueing the loss of the fish. The funny thing was that the bonefish was still in front of us and had not sped off as you would expect. It was just ambling about maybe 30 feet from the boat and Trevor jokingly said, "Have another cast," which I did, not expecting for one moment that it would take the fly, but it did! It just came up to the fly and inhaled it and once again I was into the big bonefish. We were all astonished that it had taken the fly again but, just as before, it swam around close to the boat and then came off again! I couldn't believe it. The fish still hung around afterwards and Trevor and Elias were encouraging me, yet again, to have another go for the bonefish but I decided that I would let it go on its way. After that we encountered some "normal" bonefish and caught them and then the storm hit us and that was that – what an eventful day!

On this second visit to Joulters, Trevor and I spent some time fishing for other species as well. We were having such a good week, and had caught so many big bonefish, that it was nice to spend some time fishing the deeper areas adjacent to the flats, and also around the reef, for other species such as jacks and barracuda which is always good fun and is a nice break which keeps you sharp for the bonefishing.

One of the highlights of these sessions was when I hooked a very big lemon shark that took a popper intended for barracuda. I was standing up to my knees in water at the time and the shark came out of the deeper water and had a go at the popper, but missed it. It then came back for a second time and missed it again, so I just left the popper floating on the surface a few feet in front of me and this time it came up and, amazingly, sucked it in.

I must have had the shark on for at least half an hour; I never expected to land it as I was using a light spinning rod, a fixed spool reel loaded with 15-pound line and a wire trace that was only about 20 pounds. However, after some amazingly long runs it started to look increasingly likely that the impossible would happen, and I had managed to get the shark very close to the shore when the trace went and that was that.

For the rest of the week Trevor and I focused on the bonefish, as did David and Gordon, and we continued to catch high average-sized fish which I think singles out Joulters as a superb bonefish destination. As is normally the case I caught the vast majority of bonefish on the Gotcha and only put on a different fly when fishing the turtle grass flats or dark bottomed creeks. Although it is part of the same island, fishing Joulters is vastly different from the bonefishing in the Bights and the West Side.

Anyone planning a trip to Andros might want to consider fishing all three areas if they have the time to do so, as it would be well worthwhile.

Chapter 9

Cayo Largo

Most bonefishing destinations tend to be off the beaten track, which is of course one of the main attractions, as it gives the angler the chance to get away from it all and see the world in a different light, but a fishing trip to Cuba doesn't quite fit this profile. The fishing itself is superb and the flats habitat is much as you would expect to see elsewhere, but it is the bit between getting off the plane and arriving at your chosen destination that makes Cuba so special.

The jewel in the crown is undoubtedly Havana and whenever I travel to Cuba on a bonefishing trip I make sure that I devote a couple of days to being a tourist. The city is vibrant and the bars, music and people all combine to give an unforgettable experience. During the day it is nice to just stroll around and soak up the atmosphere and culture, and it is well worth getting a guide book and swatting up on Havana before you arrive. There are some great sights to see and museums to visit that give visitors to Havana a real feel for Cuba's rich and colourful heritage and culture. By night Havana transforms itself with lively bars and great music. All of this is definitely not to be missed, so the usual trip for me to Cuba is 10 days; this gives two days in Havana on the way out and then a week's fishing followed by an overnight stop again in Havana on the way back.

On my first trip to Cuba, Trevor and I booked a week's fishing at the Casa Batida fishing lodge on Cayo Largo, which is part of the Archipiélago de los Canarreos. The archipelago forms a chain of islands that lie off the south east coast of Cuba with the largest island, Isla de la Juventud, at the far west and Cayo Largo at the eastern tip. The island of Cayo Largo is predominantly a holiday destination with several large hotels attracting visitors, mostly from Europe and Canada, in search of a holiday in the sun. The tourist beaches run along the south side of the island and are very busy throughout the main holiday periods.

In contrast to this, the flats on the north side of the island are a wonderfully tranquil haven in which to fish. They cover a vast area of superb bonefish habit that, ironically, the majority of tourists are completely unaware of and long may it continue! The fishing is controlled by the Casa Batida Fishing Club which is a well-run outfit with excellent guides. The flats have been designated by Cuba's government as a protected area, which is great to see. One can only wish and hope that other countries adopt this enlightened thinking when considering their own approach to the conservation of flats habitat.

There is no accommodation at the Casa Batida fishing lodge, so Trevor and I stayed at one of the tourist hotels, taking the short taxi ride to the Casa Batida dock each morning. This is something of a departure from staying at a usual fishing lodge with its own accommodation, but it was a welcome one, as it was good to be fishing during the day and being a holidaymaker in the evening.

My first fishing trip to Cayo Largo had many memorable moments but there are a couple that really spring to mind. The first of these was when Trevor had an 11-pound bonefish. It must have been around our third day into the fishing week with Nelson as our guide. Many of the flats at Cayo Largo are made up of hard sand or light coloured marl, but there is one very large flat, a mile or so offshore, that is solid turtle grass. The day started well enough; the cloudless sky was deep blue, there was a perfect, gentle bonefishing breeze and we soon found an enormous school of bonefish grazing over the turtle grass. Nelson slowly and quietly poled us into the ideal position to start our drift. As I was first up to fish I opened the front hatch on the skiff to put my jacket away, but just when the large and heavy hatch was fully open it slipped out of my grasp and banged shut, very loudly. The school of bonefish, which must have had a thousand fish in it, just exploded and the fish tore off in all directions, but this reaction was nothing to that of Nelson who was equally unhappy. He glared at me for the remainder of the week every time I opened one of the hatches!

Not surprisingly, those bonefish were never seen again that day but, fortunately, Nelson's humour soon returned and we were off again looking for more bonefish as we slowly poled our way across the grassy flat. It was still my turn up at the front of the boat and I started to scan the water all around. For a while we saw nothing, but then Nelson spotted a ray to our right and moved the boat in that direction to see if there was a bonefish or two following it and sure enough there was – in fact there were two and they were both good-sized fish.

Bonefish following rays is something I have witnessed many times over the years and it is always worth having a close look at a feeding ray to see if there is a bonefish just behind it, mopping up any food that has been disturbed. The best way to catch a bonefish following a ray is to cast on the back of the ray. As long as the ray is moving the fly doesn't actually land on its back and should just roll off nicely into the path of the bonefish. A small crab pattern can be very effective and is often eagerly taken.

As I needed to redeem myself with Nelson after dropping the hatch cover, I made sure my first cast landed in the right spot on the back of the ray. One of the bonefish had it straight away, but it was the smaller of the two fish. Despite this, I knew it was a good one and it tore off picking up loads of turtle grass on the way, which made playing the fish both difficult and nerve-racking but eventually I landed a very fit looking bonefish of 8 pounds which at the time was my best from Cuba.

After a quick photo, we slipped the fish back, Trevor took his place at the front of the boat and we commenced our drift, but we didn't see anything for what seemed an age. The arrangement that Trevor and I have is that we each take 30-minute turns to fish whilst the skiff is being poled and Trevor must have been about 29 minutes into his shift when another ray turned up, but this time it had one very big bonefish in tow. Once again Nelson manoeuvred the boat into the correct position and Trevor put the fly nicely on the back of the ray and, as with the earlier fish, it was taken first time.

Up until this point I had never caught or witnessed a genuine double-digit bonefish, but it was immediately apparent that Trevor had hooked a very big fish. It wasn't so much that the runs this particular bonefish made were much faster or longer than other bonefish, the main difference was that it wouldn't come in. It had initially done three very long runs but after the third it stayed maybe 50 yards away and just circled the boat for what felt like forever and, as with my earlier fish, had accumulated stacks of weed on the line. We were all worried that the added pressure from the weed would either pull out the hook or break the line. Another worry was that although the turtle grass flat looked harmless enough, the grass was growing out of rock and coral. Trevor's line was being weighed down by the grass hanging from it and it was difficult for him to keep the line out of the water so we all feared that the line might catch on the coral and break.

Cayo Largo

Eventually, after a very long time, the bonefish started to come ever closer to the boat and finally Nelson used his net to lift on board the first double-digit bonefish that either Trevor or I had seen. What was also evident was Nelson's delight at the fish and it's always a good sign when your guide, who must see thousands of bonefish over the course of a year, also gets excited!

The fish had fought for a long time and we wanted to get it back in the water so, after a quick measurement and photo, we returned it and it swam away strongly. The fish weighed just over 11 pounds and it was good for both of us to get a double-digit bonefish in the boat after many years of trying. The drinks were on Trevor that evening!

The other interesting event that week concerned fishing muds, which is where you get many hundreds, perhaps thousands of bonefish, shoaled up together and because they are feeding hard they create a large area of cloudy water or a "mud". Trevor and I had met John in Havana on the way out to Cayo Largo. John was a retired vet from East Sussex and was delightful company. He also made a great play about how old he was, that his eyesight was poor, he couldn't cast and that he needed to take an hour-long nap at midday, either on the boat or on an island if he could find one, in order to make it through the arduous bonefishing day.

Now Trevor and I pride ourselves at being pretty capable bonefishers and whenever we fished out of a lodge we would try to be one of the top boats for the week and, although we didn't always get there, we would be pretty close. On our first day we returned to the Casa Batida dock having had 14 bonefish between us and we felt good about this. Everyone else had caught less than us, but John had caught 23 and had his midday nap too! This routine continued throughout the week; Trevor and I caught plenty of bonefish, regularly securing second spot, so to speak, but John came in every day, refreshed from his midday sleep, having caught at least 20 bonefish.

By Friday, Trevor and I had had enough. We instructed Nelson that we must catch more than John so, with some reluctance, he took us in a new direction that was a good 30-minute boat ride offshore and put us on a deepish flat that appeared to go on forever. Nelson didn't pole initially, but just motored around slowly, looking intently for something. The "something" turned out to be a huge area of cloudy water which was the biggest mud Trevor and I had ever seen, it must have been 100 yards in diameter.

It was clear that Nelson disliked fishing muds because they are too easy and this is a view I now share, but on this particular day we just wanted to catch more than John! Nelson positioned the skiff just up tide of the mud and having secured the boat to the push pole we were ready for the off. Because of the size of the mud it was possible for both Trevor and I to fish from the boat at the same time and we started to catch one bonefish after another. By lunchtime we had caught more than 20 bonefish, with some good ones too, plus a few jacks which added a little variety. It was also about this time that John turned up and he was a little disappointed to find that we had pinched his bonefish mud. It was now clear to us how he had managed to catch so many fish throughout the earlier part of the week. By the time we packed up, Trevor and I had caught 57 bonefish between us, but John still managed to catch 23 and he even made time for his afternoon nap! He may have been well into his seventies and perhaps his eyesight may have not been what it once was, but there was nothing wrong with his casting and he was clearly a very capable bonefisher.

I'm pleased I fished the mud that day; firstly because Trevor and I managed, at long last, to catch more that John, but secondly because it got fishing a mud out of my system. I have not fished a mud since then and although I really enjoyed catching so many bonefish that day it proved to me that the aspect I enjoy most about bonefishing is the opportunity it gives for stalking and sight fishing which is so lacking when fishing a mud. Having said that, everyone who goes bonefishing should fish a mud at least once. They should enjoy the experience and not feel too precious about it when they do.

That first week I spent at Cayo Largo was probably one of the most enjoyable bonefishing trips I had had up until then and it was certainly the most productive in terms of numbers of fish. The average size was also very good and, in addition to Trevor's 11 pounder, we had many other fish that week at around the 7- and 8-pound mark.

A Bonefishing Journey

Another plus point was the variety of species that inhabit Cayo Largo which is in contrast to the Bahamian islands where bonefish tend to be the dominant species. In addition to the bonefish, Trevor and I had plenty of tarpon, jacks, snapper and barracuda, which are always a welcome addition. Not surprisingly, I have returned to Cayo Largo on a couple more occasions and the fishing has never disappointed, with consistent catches of better than average-sized bonefish and with the bonus of landing fish of other species.

As in the Bahamas, the Gotcha reigns supreme in Cayo Largo; when fishing the sandy and marl flats I use it all the time and have seen no reason to alter this approach. The only consideration is whether to use bead eyes or heavier lead eyes and this will be determined by the water depth. At the Casa Batida lodge they recommend a Gotcha tied with a yellow head rather than the more usual pink, but I have not found this to make any difference and continue to use Gotchas tied in the conventional way.

The one other fly I use here is the Bonefish Bitters, which I have found particularly effective on the turtle grass flats. As is often the case, orange has worked best for me and, of course, a weed guard is essential to prevent continually hooking up on the turtle grass.

Whatever fly is used, it is mandatory at Casa Batida to use a barbless hook which is good to see and, once again, is an indication of the conservationist approach that Cuba takes towards bonefishing.

As a bonefishing destination, there is an interesting diversity of habit at Cayo Largo with inside and outside flats, creeks, hard sand flats, grassy flats and deeper marl bottomed areas that all contain high numbers of bonefish. There are many mangrove islands with their incumbent channels and lagoons which enhance the fishing experience and give the opportunity to fish for other species such as tarpon, jacks and snapper.

The Casa Batida Fishing Club is a professionally run operation with well-maintained skiffs and capable guides, although an ability to speak some Spanish will come in handy as not all the guides are fluent in English. The fishing is split into zones and conservation measures insist that these zones are not fished every day, which undoubtedly helps improve the fishing. As a bonefish destination Cayo Largo, and the Casa Batida Fishing Club, are exceptional and well worth a visit.

Chapter 10

Cayo Coco

Cayo Coco was a bit of a gamble. Sue and I were going to spend a week there and I was fully kitted out with all my bonefishing tackle and clothing that had tested the flight baggage allowance to the limit. For the first time I had not booked a guide and, even more intriguingly, did not even know if there was any serious guide programme on the island. So it was destined to be an interesting week!

The island of Cayo Coco is very similar to Cayo Largo in that it is primarily a holiday destination; it is situated off the north coast of Cuba and is part of the Archipiélago Jardines del Rey. I had, of course, done plenty of web research and knew there were bonefish present, I had also managed to obtain the names of some of the local fishermen who supposedly took out anglers to fish the flats. However, after checking in to the hotel in Cayo Coco my enquires at the hotel reception met with blank expressions from the staff, so I knew that I would have to move quickly, or have a slice of luck, if I was to get some fishing in before the end of the week.

Cayo Coco

The slice of luck came in the shape of Bruce, Ron and Rob who were three Canadian bonefishers staying in the hotel. It was on our second day and Sue and I were on our way to breakfast when she said, "Three bonefishers, 50 feet at 10 o'clock!". I looked over and sure enough there they were, three guys all decked out in their bonefishing finery complete with rods and bags. Sue and I quickly made a detour so that I could have a chat with them and find out if they knew the whereabouts of a bonefish guide. The great thing about bonefishing is that when you meet another bonefisher you can immediately strike up a relationship, and this is exactly what happened. Within minutes, Bruce had invited me to share a boat and guide with him the following day; Ron and Rob would be in a second boat. So my worries about finding a guide had just disappeared and I had also found three new bonefishing friends – perfect!

The following morning all four of us were back in reception waiting to be picked up by taxi which would take us to the bonefishing dock, where we would meet our guide. Of course this was Cuban time and it took a phone call or two to galvanise our promised taxi, but it did finally arrive, though rather later than expected! The journey, which took about half an hour, was highly entertaining and took us through some real wilderness areas that the usual tourists never see, adding yet another dimension to the day. The drive also involved crossing a bridge that was severely damaged and which looked in danger of falling down at any moment. I clearly remember crossing my fingers each time we went over it.

Our destination was a small dock on Cayo Romano, which is an extensive area of flats adjacent to Cayo Coco. Bruce and I met up with our guide Duniesky and before too long we were on our way. Once again I experienced that tremendous feeling of excitement that accompanies any first day's bonefishing at a new destination. The only downside was the weather; the sky was getting darker by the minute and the wind stronger and I sensed we would be in for a challenging day. We did stop briefly on the way to the flats to have a go at some tarpon that we had spotted in one of the channels, but as so often happens when fishing for tarpon they only briefly showed themselves before effortlessly disappearing again. After that we resumed our journey and by the time Duniesky finally slid the boat onto what looked an enormous flat the weather had really turned grim. The strong wind, which had been steadily building, was now accompanied by persistent rain – such is bonefishing!

It is at times like this that good wet weather gear really comes in to its own, so on went my three-layer Gore-Tex jacket with the hood up and firmly tied down. I never go on a bonefish flat without it, as it is impossible to know what the weather will do. Bruce and I began slowly wading our way across the flat, but it was difficult to see much due to the strong winds and lack of sun. The rain just compounded the situation and I had to continually stop to clean my Polaroid glasses. The morning, not surprisingly, was unproductive and by lunchtime neither of us had caught a thing. However, I had seen three very big bonefish that wouldn't have looked out of place on the West Side of Andros and I was encouraged by this. The weather on that first day never changed, but I did manage to catch one bonefish of no great size from a channel and lose another. So I had broken my duck and caught my first bonefish from the northern shoreline of Cuba. I did, however, see several bonefish during the day, through my steamed up Polaroids, and they looked very big indeed, which was encouraging. What was even more interesting was that when we got back to the dock we found that Ron and Rob had caught an 8- and 9-pound bonefish respectively, which proved that there were very big bonefish present and that my sightings hadn't been exaggerated.

The weather remained pretty grim the next day so all four of us, and Sue, stayed at the hotel and swapped bonefish stories. The following day, however, dawned bright and sunny and we were more eager than ever to go fishing again! As before, I shared a boat with Bruce, with Duniesky as our guide, and he took us to the same flat we fished the first day. I was happy about this as I wanted to have another chance to catch one of the big bonefish I had briefly spotted during the rain storm. It was amazing how different things looked now, with the sun shining from a clear blue sky; the murky grey water that we had endured before had become bright and crystal clear and it was impossible to believe we were in the same place. The perfect conditions meant that if one of the big bonefish did appear then there would be a good chance that we would see it.

Something I have noticed over the years, and I don't know why this happens, is that more often than not when the skiff is parked up and you are about to start fishing, bonefish appear on the scene soon afterwards. Perhaps this is just curiosity on their part and they are attracted by the noise of the skiff but, no sooner had I stepped over the side of the boat, than three good-sized bonefish suddenly appeared. They were just too far away to cast to, but this gave me time to strip off enough line and compose myself. By the time I had done this they were in range, I got off my first cast and the Gotcha landed about 5 feet to the right of the lead fish. I expected the fish to see the fly, but it seemed totally unaware that the fly was there resting on the bottom. I gave the fly a short 6-inch pull and one of the other fish darted out and inhaled the fly – they certainly were hungry bonefish!

The bonefish was a good one, as were all three, and it shot off at lightning speed. I always know when I have hooked a big bone as I start to worry about running out of backing. It is very doubtful that this will ever happen as I put 200 yards of 30-pound backing on my reels, but these big fish do get well into it! This particular fish put up a good fight and took quite an age to get in. I finally grabbed the leader and managed to lift enough of its head out of the water, to prevent it getting away, before slipping my hand under what was a very fit and healthy looking 8 pounder – what a great start to the day.

After a quick photo we continued wading and shortly after another small pod came into view. Once again I was soon hooked up to another good fish, eventually landing an even bigger bonefish of 9 pounds. Fish of this size don't come along very often and to catch two big bonefish in short succession was very special – and they were caught wading, too, which is always a bonus!

Both Bruce and I were convinced we were in for an amazing day, but after that brief flurry of activity we didn't see another bonefish for some time. It wasn't until midday that Bruce spotted a small pod of bonefish and finally broke his duck with a fish around the 5-pound mark. I was pleased about this because there is nothing worse than one angler catching all the fish whilst the other remains fishless. Up until that point Bruce was beginning to get a little despondent, but he needn't have worried as he was destined for a very memorable afternoon's fishing, as in fact we both were!

After a brief stop for lunch, we moved on to another flat and started to wade. Initially there were no fish to be seen and I was beginning to think that we would finish up with just the three bonefish. The flat we were fishing, unlike the one we fished before lunch which was unbroken white sand, had quite large clumps of weed that covered the bottom in some areas. Looking out across the flat gave the impression of a mosaic of white and green.

After wading for maybe an hour, and convincing myself that that we wouldn't see any more bonefish, I briefly spotted a very large fish about 50 yards away. It moved out of one of the green weed areas, crossed a small, white sandy patch and then went into another green area – and it was a very big fish!

As I slowly made my way towards the green patch the bonefish had moved on to, my eyes were glued to the white sandy area that surrounded it as I knew that at some point the fish would once again come into view. Eventually, I was within casting range of the green patch that contained my big bonefish, so after checking my fly, leader and drag tension on the reel, I stood perfectly still and waited. Bonefish are always on the move and I knew that sooner or later the bonefish would re-emerge from the sanctuary of the green, weedy patch. Sure enough it did and it looked enormous. The white sandy patch was perhaps 20 feet wide and, as the bonefish slowly began making its way across it, I cast about 10 feet in front of it, waited for a few seconds and then moved the Gotcha just a few inches before finally letting it come to rest.

Like the fish I had taken during the morning, this bonefish was hungry and hammered into the fly and I found myself attached to a very big bonefish which streaked off at an even faster speed than the 9 pounder I had landed earlier. It made the customary three very long runs that I had come to expect from a big bonefish but then, just like Trevor's big bonefish from Cayo Largo, it stayed about

50 yards away, continually circling me for what seemed forever and just wouldn't come in. By this time Bruce had joined me and we stood and watched as the bonefish put up a very spirited resistance. I knew that as long as the leader was not damaged, and assuming it was a good hook hold and providing I didn't do anything rash, then I would land the fish, which I did.

Up until then I hadn't caught a double-digit bonefish. I had landed quite a few 9 pounders from various locations and had seen Trevor's big fish, but today I realised my my overriding bonefish ambition to catch a 10 pounder. In fact, it was 10 pounds 2 ounces. I was a very contented angler and would happily buy the mojitos that evening!

If we caught nothing else that day I wouldn't have worried, but Bruce had had a very lean time up until this point and it would round off a good day if he could catch a decent bonefish. With an hour or so left to fish we jumped back in boat and headed off towards another flat that Duniesky wanted us to try.

It struck me at that moment that Duniesky was one of those guides who works you hard. He was eager to catch fish in his boat and hadn't tired of catching bonefish, tarpon and permit. He didn't like to spend much time over lunch and was keen to move on to the next flat once the existing one had stopped producing. Guides like this are great fun to fish with and invariably the fishing is more productive as a result of their enthusiasm – as would soon be demonstrated.

The next flat turned out to be nothing like the previous ones. It was knee deep and covered, for the most part, in unusually dark green turtle grass. The only exception to this was a very weird V-shaped formation of sand in the middle of the flat. Each arm of the V was about 200 yards in length and about 30 yards at its widest point, and the sand was pure white which made a stark contrast to the surrounding dense, dark green turtle grass. Bruce and I each took an arm of the V, I opted for the right-hand one and Bruce and Duniesky took the left.

I had just started making my way up the right arm when a bonefish emerged on to the sand in front of me, about 100 yards away. It was travelling towards me, so I stayed put and waited for it to come into casting range. I soon found myself attached to another good-sized bone. The fish shot across to my left and on to Bruce's stretch of sand, so I moved in the same direction to try to get better control over the fish. It was exactly at this point that Duniesky started to get very excited, pointing towards the far end of the sandbar that I had been fishing. There, at the far end, were five, very big dark shapes and they were clearly permit!

By now I was standing in Bruce's part of the V still playing my bonefish, so Bruce and Duniesky quickly made their way around me and then up the right-hand of the V towards the permit. Bruce was using only an 8 weight rod, so that would have to do, and I could see Duniesky hurriedly tying on a crab pattern for him. Permit, as we know, are fickle creatures at the best of times and having cast to them myself, and watched them refuse the fly and also seen the same thing happen time and again to other anglers, I wasn't expecting much of a result. I focused back on the bonefish and soon landed another nice fish of 6 pounds. This last fish meant that I had caught four bonefish with a total weight of 33 pounds. This gave an average weight of just over 8 pounds which is remarkably high and just showed what the north coast of Cuba is capable of producing.

After landing the bonefish I eventually looked up to see that the permit, with Bruce with Duniesky in tow, had moved off the white sand and they were now 50 yards into the dark green turtle grass. Duniesky was continually pointing at the permit whilst giving instructions to Bruce, who would then cast in the required direction. I was feeling very content having caught four good bonefish, so was happy to stand and watch and really didn't expect anything to happen, when suddenly Bruce's 8 weight rod arched over – he was into a permit!

I must have been standing about 200 yards away from the action, so I slowly waded towards them in water that, by now, came up to my thighs. As I made my way over the sands I just kept thinking how marvellous it would be if Bruce could actually land the permit. It would definitely round off what had already been an exceptional day's fishing. This would also be my first opportunity to see a permit close up.

By the time I got to Bruce and Duniesky they both had completely different expressions on their faces. Duniesky was grinning from ear to ear, thoroughly enjoying the moment. Bruce had that worried look that I guess all anglers suffer from when they are fortunate enough to hook a big permit. The permit was doing its utmost to keep him in a state of heightened tension! It was putting up a really solid resistance and having done a number of searing, lengthy runs it was now holding in the current some way off. Although it would allow itself to be drawn in maybe 10 yards closer it would, with what seemed just a flick of its tail, make up the 10 yards and be back on station. This carried on for quite a while and then slowly the permit begrudgingly began to give ground. Eventually Bruce had the fish close enough to see it clearly and it was indeed a very big permit. By this time Bruce must have been playing the permit for about half an hour which gave me the opportunity to take many shots of him playing the fish as it came ever closer. At one point, Duniesky was just about ready to grab the permit's tail when it suddenly shot off at lightning speed on another 100-yard run. Bruce let out a groan of frustration, as he knew he was in for another bout of sparring with the permit. The tension on Bruce's face was really starting to show!

Another 15 minutes passed and then once again the permit was very close. Eventually, after a couple of near misses, Duniesky finally grabbed a still very lively and very big permit by the tail. Bruce had caught his permit and

The Girls Flat, Harbour Island at low tide.

Fishing for tailers on Harbour Island.

Fishing for bonefish with Jack Aley from the road in Harbour Island.

The big storm on Harbour Island.

Fishing for a bonefish close to the boat.

A big Cayo Largo bonefish caught off the back of a ray.

Who knows what the day will bring?   *Below: Cuban mangroves.*

David Keens with a good-size Cuban tarpon. Below: A nice Ascension Bay snook.

My big Cayo Coco bonefish. *Below: Manuel Chac's boat.*

The day begins at Ascension Bay, Mexico.

Another bone falls to the Gotcha.

Gotchas come in all weights and sizes.

would definitely be buying the mojitos that evening – and maybe for the rest of the week! The permit was a wonderful creature and I was taken by its huge eyes. Bruce was overjoyed by the capture and had done very well to land such a big permit on an 8 weight rod and 10-pound leader. We didn't weigh the permit, but all agreed it was somewhere around the 30-pound mark, which is more than big enough. I then took some more photos before we released the fish and watched it swim away very strongly.

The boat ride back was great; both Bruce and I were very happy with our day's fishing as was Duniesky. The elation carried on into the small hours until, overdosed on mojitos and incapable of elaborating any more on how to catch 30-pound permit or 10-pound bonefish to Sue, Ron and Rob, we called it a day.

I didn't fish any more during the remainder of the week and haven't been back to Cayo Coco since, but certainly will do. On reflection, although it has many parallels with Cayo Largo in that it is an island chain and flats area of comparable size and is also a holiday destination, it is a different type fishery, though this may change with time.

At the moment Cayo Coco lacks the sheer numbers of bonefish that are evident on the south coast of Cuba. However, it more than makes up for this in terms of quality and therefore should be a serious consideration for trophy- sized bonefish. The relatively small numbers of large bonefish may be the result of local netting of the area. There are tales of huge catches having been taken this way but it appears that the netting has, thankfully, now ceased and the area is a designated protected fishery. If this is the case, then it is indeed enlightened thinking and should be applauded. I can see Cayo Coco becoming a superb bonefishing destination in the years to come.

Chapter 11

Punta Allen

Travelling to a new saltwater fly fishing destination is always an exciting prospect as there is much to look forward to. I try not to arrive with too many preconceived ideas, but I find it very difficult not to speculate about a fishing trip in the weeks and months beforehand. What will the flats be like? How big are the bonefish likely to be and in what numbers? What will the lodge be like and how good are the guides? What about the weather? These, of course, were just a few of the many imponderables I was mulling over as I sat in Manchester Airport having just sent my groaning kit bag, that was just a few ounces light of the baggage allowance, on its way to the hold. And there begs another question – would it arrive in Cancun?

Very rarely are these preconceptions anything like the reality and this was certainly the case with my first trip to fish the Ascension Bay region in Mexico. By rights, Chris and I should not have been sitting in the departure lounge in Manchester Airport en route to Mexico. My original plan, earlier in the year, was to return to the north coast of Cuba. My last trip there had been very productive and I wanted to capitalize on what I had learnt with another trip, but I had found it impossible to contact my guide – all my efforts via email and phone had proved fruitless, as is often the case in Cuba. The final straw was when the flight operator changed its winter timetable so I couldn't fly direct from the UK into Cayo Coco. I therefore abandoned all hope of a trip to Cuba and booked a week's fishing in Mexico at the last minute.

This change of location, from Cuba to Mexico, was not a difficult one. I had fished my way around the Caribbean for over 10 years and had constantly speculated about a trip to Mexico, but other destinations in the Bahamas and Cuba always seemed to get in the way, so I regarded this as an opportunity to put that right. We were on our way to the small town of Punta Allen which lies at the very tip of a long peninsula jutting out into Ascension Bay. I was looking forward to fishing some new flats and the chance to experience the Mexican culture.

The flight over was trouble-free and happily all the rods and reels arrived safely in Cancun. At the airport Chris and I met up with Hilary, Steve, Jonathan and Paul who would also be staying at the fishing lodge during the coming week. I have always been very fortunate in the people I have met whilst on bonefishing trips and it was clear from the outset that we all had a similar sense of humour and would get on well, which is important and adds to the overall fishing experience.

Punta Allen

The journey to the lodge was by taxi and our driver was Rupert. Past experience has taught me to expect taxis in all sorts of sizes and degrees of roadworthiness, but I was pleasantly surprised to see that Rupert's taxi was new and easily accommodated the six of us plus our entire luggage – and it had the added avantage of being air conditioned! By the time we set off it was about five in the afternoon and the plan was to drive to Tulum which was about an hour away. We planned to stop there for something to eat and then continue on to Punta Allen.

The drive to Tulum was soon over and we relaxed in a restaurant for an hour or so, getting to know one another and discussing the fishing. The meal was my first experience of genuine Mexican food and it was very, very hot. We started off with salsa and tortillas and the salsa was off the Richter scale in terms of heat. I needed three bottles of ice-cold Corona just to get me in some sort of shape to be able to eat the main course which was excellent and, thankfully, slightly less challenging in terms of heat.

Once the meal was over we eagerly resumed our journey. The distance from the airport to Tulum, around 70 miles, had taken us just over an hour and with only another 30 miles to go I was confident we would soon be in Punta Allen – how wrong I was!

The first 10 miles to Punta Allen was relatively speedy and uneventful, but things rapidly took a downturn when we arrived at the rainforest reserve. As we entered the reserve we had to stop at a small building where a guard insisted that we sign some sort of document before continuing on our journey. Chris volunteered for this task, although none of us understood the nature of the document or its purpose – let's hope it doesn't come back to haunt him in the future!

The signing ceremony wasted a good 15 minutes which, having already spent over 20 hours travelling, was an irritant we could have done without. We eventually resumed our journey, but no sooner had we got up to speed when the road just seemed to disappear – or to be precise, it turned into an endless series of giant potholes. The road had at one point been a proper road with a tarmac surface, but this had been worn or washed away through bad weather, poor maintenance and continued use. The path of the road was still there, but the drive was exceedingly uncomfortable as we were all jolted this way and that as we entered and exited the never-ending procession of potholes. I remember at one point someone saying that it was the only road they had travelled on that had riffles and pools! Ironically, and just to heighten passenger irritation, the original road had been built with speed bumps and these were the only parts of the original surface that remained!

While we were in the rainforest, the journey in the dark was quite eerie. Just to make matters slightly worse we were stopped by half a dozen soldiers who were fully armed and kitted out in battle fatigues – just what we needed. They emerged out of the jungle about two hours into our bumpy journey and glared at us all in turn through the driver's open window. We later found out they were after drug runners, but as we didn't fit the bill they let us continue on our way – thankfully.

The journey from the entrance to the rainforest to Punta Allen took just over three and a half hours, averaging about 8 miles per hour over the very uncomfortable terrain. I had spent the final hour wishing and willing a "Welcome to Punta Allen" sign to emerge from the gloom and eventually saw a small light glittering in the undergrowth ahead and then another and all of a sudden there were buildings, lights, noise and Punta Allen.

After such a journey it's easy to wish that there had been a dual carriage way all the way from Tulum to Punta Allen, with perhaps somewhere to stop and buy a beer and take a leak along the way, but if it were like this then Punta Allen and its isolated bonefishing wouldn't exist. Instead, there would be the great big tourist hotels and shops, so in a way I am glad the dodgy road is there to preserve, what I would discover over the week, is a very special small fishing village on the edge of an important and preserved rainforest.

The lodge we were staying at was the Casa Viejo Chac which is run by Manuel Chac and, despite the late hour of our arrival, the welcoming committee was out in full to greet us, which was good to see. Manuel, of course was there organizing our luggage to be taken from us and offering a tray of cold beers. Our guides for the week, Tara and Pablo, along with Marbella and Pepe, who would provide us with great breakfasts, lunches and dinner throughout our visit, were also part of the welcome group. Although I had never stayed at the lodge before, or met Manuel, it became immediately clear to me, even at the late hour of arrival and with its accompanying fatigue, that Casa Viejo Chac was clearly a well-run and welcoming lodge. It would undoubtedly be a great place to spend a week saltwater fly fishing. By now the uncomfortable road journey was becoming a distant memory and I was starting to look forward to the following morning's fishing with eager anticipation.

Over the beers we had decided as a group that rather than fish with the same guide all week we would rotate guides which is something I have increasingly grown to like. Guides often have their own favourite areas they like to fish and guide in different ways, and I find fishing with different guides adds to the overall variety of the fishing.

The first morning dawned bright and sunny, in fact it was perfect weather for saltwater fly fishing, and Chris and I were to be guided by Tara. Something that I had not encountered before and which appears unique to this region, is that each boat has two guides rather than one. The way this works is that each boat has a head guide, in this case Tara, and a younger, junior guide who is learning the ropes and will eventually become a head guide at some time in the future. This arrangement is treated very seriously by all guides, senior and junior, and it was clear from the onset that Elmer, our junior guide for the day and who was only about 16 years old, was a very accomplished guide in his own right. The obvious great advantage with having two guides is that when wading, each angler can go off in different directions whilst still having the services of a dedicated guide.

One other difference that immediately became apparent is that the guides don't fish from conventional skiffs, but use much bigger boats that are 24 feet long – they reminded me of the boats I fished out of in Los Roques. Although much larger, they still have a poling platform at the back and a casting area up front.

Over the course of the week it was possible to compare these Ascension Bay type boats to the conventional skiffs used throughout the Bahamas and Cuba; there were advantages and disadvantages on both sides. On the plus side, I found the larger boats far more comfortable and this was especially so when crossing the large expanse of Ascension Bay which becomes pretty choppy when there is a wind blowing. The casting area was also far better; it was bigger and had a raised area around it that sheltered the fly line and stopped it being blown overboard, as often happens in conventional skiffs when it is very windy.

The one big downside I found with the Ascension Bay boats was the wave noise they created when poling – there would be a noticeable slap as each wave came up against the side of the boat. As a result it was difficult to get really close to the fish, which meant there was a constant need for long casts; skiffs in comparison are much quieter and can get you closer to your quarry. However, as most of the fishing during the week was done whilst wading, it really wasn't too much of a problem.

That first morning, when Tara asked me what I wanted to fish for, it struck me that this was a question rarely asked by a guide in the Bahamas, simply because the dominant species there is, without doubt, the bonefish. Ascension Bay, by contrast, is a fishing destination where bonefish, permit, tarpon and, as I was to find out during the course of that first day, snook, all exist in abundance. And for this reason the fishery should be regarded as very much a mixed saltwater fly fishing destination, instead of solely a bonefish destination. Despite this, my answer to Tara was that we should fish for bonefish, as it would be an easier option compared to the demands and stress I always associate with permit fishing! Catching a few fish on the first day is always important, as it gets the week off to a good start.

After getting everything loaded in the boat we set off at speed across Ascension Bay towards the islands and creeks on the other side of the bay. I did, indeed, catch some bonefish and Chris, who was on his first saltwater trip, had also caught a couple by lunchtime, which we were both pleased about.

By early afternoon, having fished a number of different spots, we motored up towards a shoreline where the mangrove roots hung vertically into a foot or so of water.

Punta Allen

No sooner had we stopped than we noticed a couple of biggish snook, lying up in amongst the mangrove roots. Snook are one of those fish I have caught now and again, but they were by no means common in the places I fished in the Bahamas or Cuba, so an opportunity to catch one was very appealing. The only problem was that no matter how much Chris and I tried they would not come out from behind the mangrove cover to take our flies, so after a while Tara started to pole us further along the shoreline.

We must have gone a couple of hundred yards when suddenly a couple of snook appeared in open water and then, just about the same time, the water erupted further along the shore as a huge school of mullet leapt in unison as yet more snook chased them. For the next hour we had some superb fishing for snook in the open water and I caught four good fish, all between 7 and 10 pounds, and Chris also had a 10 pounder. Despite the feeding frenzy that was going on, they were surprisingly picky when it came to the fly and the retrieve, and only seemed interested in a white and chartreuse deceiver fished in very fast short strips. Once I settled on this it proved deadly and in addition to the fish caught, Chris and I both lost other snook and had many follows – and all this was going on in water just a foot deep so it was very visual and exciting.

My next chance of catching some snook came a couple of days later. Manuel was our guide for the day and, as I had anticipated, we went to a completely different area of Ascension Bay that runs along the mainland shore on the edge of the rainforest. Although the morning had been slow, I had picked up another decent snook of perhaps 8 pounds. The weather then began to turn increasingly cloudy and there were heavy rainstorms gathering on the horizon, so an early finish was on the cards. By mid-afternoon we were poling close to shore, Chris was up front on the casting deck and it was my turn to sit it out in the boat. The clouds were even more menacing by now, the horizon was almost black and coming our way, so I was certain that this would be our last bit of fishing for the day. Rather than just sit and watch Chris, I decided to get out of the boat and wade fish the nearby mangroves and let the boat continue on its path. They could come back for me when they were done.

The mangroves by the shore looked an ideal location for snook with plenty of cover for them to hide in. I started wading about 10 yards out from the shoreline and, sure enough, I soon spotted a good fish amongst the mangrove roots, but it was well hidden and certainly wasn't keen to emerge from its lair. I continued slowly, wading ever closer to the shore, and for a while didn't see a thing. There was a slight point to the shoreline a little further ahead, so I decided I would continue in that direction before calling it a day. By the time I reached the point, I was just about ready to wind in and make my way back to Manuel and the boat, when I spotted two very big snook lying perfectly still just a few yards ahead of me. In fact I nearly trod on them and only saw them at the very last minute. The snook, lying parallel to each other were, fortunately, facing away from me. As I had been wading slowly and quietly they hadn't detected my presence.

Both snook were well into double figures and considerably bigger than anything else I had caught or spotted up until now. They were so close to me that I only needed to roll cast to reach them, so I placed my deceiver just to right of the snook. The instant the fly hit the water the right-hand fish turned towards it and then lunged on it as soon as I moved the fly. It would have been nice if I could have described its capture but, after a lengthy and gritty encounter, the snook cleared the water with one final head-shaking leap and the fly just dropped out. I would have liked to have landed the snook and although I'm not going to estimate its possible weight, I will say that it was much, much bigger than the 10 pounder I had taken on the first day. Still, it just proved to me how big the snook in Ascension Bay can be and this encounter only reinforced my desire to come back for another go. I suspect that snook could well be territorial and hang around their favourite mangrove, so if that is the case I know where the big snook lives!

The permit fishing throughout the week was, for me, similar to all the other encounters I have had with the species, in that I had a few casts at them but didn't catch any! Each time I come across permit they are always charging around, constantly changing direction – if they would just stay still long enough for me to get a fly in front of them I feel sure I would have some success. That didn't happen, so I will just keep on trying, but I did leave Ascension Bay having seen more permit than in other saltwater destinations and I had a feeling that this is a good a place as any to target permit.

The other species that figures prominently in Ascension Bay is tarpon but, apart from catching one small one, I saw very few during the week. In truth Chris and I didn't target areas where you would normally expect to catch them; with so many different species to go for, it is impossible to fish for them all. As we were fishing in November I expected to see less tarpon than in May or June and I'm sure that at that time of year there would be far more tarpon to be caught.

Last but not least there are the bonefish and here, once again, my preconceptions were to be proved wrong. I had arrived in Mexico expecting to see very few, if any, large bonefish and that the average size would be very small, but this wasn't the case. The size of bonefish was never going to match those of Cuba or Andros, but they were certainly bigger than I had anticipated and compared well to places like Eleuthera and Long Island.

There were, of course, plenty of small bonefish to be caught and Chris, as someone new to bonefishing, quite rightly spent some time casting and fishing for them and learning his trade. These small bonefish were in immense schools which were usually found within the quieter bays and inlets. However, it soon became apparent that the larger bonefish, either singles or in small pods, were outside of the bays and patrolled to the shoreline. These fish averaged over 3 pounds and I had a few to over 4 pounds. I also saw bonefish a lot bigger than this and it would be interesting to discover how big some of these bonefish actually are. This requires a targeted effort on the part of the angler, but I found this difficult at Ascension Bay because of all the distractions from other species, such as permit, tarpon and snook!

As well as the fishing, I found the wildlife around Ascension Bay surprisingly diverse. Seeing a variety of birds, mammals and reptiles is always an important and rewarding element to any bonefishing trip, but Ascension Bay was very special in this respect. Of particular note were the alligators, some of which grow quite large; we also had sightings of manatee which is not something you normally encounter. The bird life was equally diverse, so a day's fishing is interesting even if you don't catch much.

As with all saltwater fly fishing trips this one came and went all too quickly. The variety of the fishing was a pleasant surprise and the lodge first class. The only part of the week I wasn't looking forward to was the return journey back to the airport along the bumpy road, but heavy rain on the last fishing day of the week damaged the road further, so it was impossible to use it. This meant a different route back that was partly by boat, and although the journey was longer in terms of miles covered, the roads were better and this proved a faster, more comfortable route in the end. Let's hope the bumpy road stays that way and preserves Punta Allen just the way it is, so that fly fishers can continue to experience the first-class fishing it offers and the hospitality of its people.

Chapter 12

Bonefish Stuff

It's probably fair to say that I have had almost as much pleasure buying bonefishing gear over the years as I have had actually catching the fish itself – bonefishing must be a dream come true for the fishing tackle trade! However, being properly kitted out so that you can fish effectively is hugely important when bonefishing and will certainly result in catching more fish.

Buying the right equipment is essential for anyone who is seriously considering taking up bonefishing. This falls into three categories: the tackle you fish with, what you wear when you are bonefishing and, finally, all the other bits and pieces that you need on a bonefish trip.

The two most obvious items of essential tackle are the rods and reels. I have used the plural for both, because of the need to cope with the variety of weather conditions that can be experienced over a week-long bonefishing trip – one day it will be flat calm and require lighter tackle, whereas on very windy days a heavier set up will be necessary.

When I first started bonefishing the selection of saltwater fly fishing rods was limited, but over the last decade some excellent specialist rods have been brought onto the market. Not only are many of these rods first-class fishing tools, but the majority are of four piece construction which is essential to the travelling angler. Typical bonefishing rods will be 9 feet in length and designed to handle lines in the AFTM 7, 8 and 9 ranges, which will cover most situations. The 7 weight models will be suitable for those bonefish destinations where the fish don't grow particularly big, but the 8 and 9 weight rods will prove ideal for bigger bonefish and the latter will be needed for casting larger flies, especially in windy conditions. It is these two rod weights that I use for the majority of my bonefishing. I have used a 7 weight for destinations where the bonefish were smaller, but found that regardless of the size of bonefish the wind still blows the same, so I now just take 8 and 9 weight rods on trips. In fact, I take two 8 weight rods, which is the rod weight I use most of the time, just in case one breaks which has happened to me on a couple of occasions.

The actual make and model chosen will be very much down to the individual angler, but some of the main factors to take into consideration will be casting style, how good the rod is to fish with, its durability and your budget. It is worth remembering when deciding what rods to purchase, that the rod will need to perform a variety of tasks. The first is a fairly obvious one in that the rod should able to cast well and, as I have already mentioned, this should suit the angler's own preferred casting style and capability. Not only should the rod be able to cast a long line, but it should also be capable of casting well at short range which is often called for when bonefishing. Some rods that have a very fast action will be fine at casting a long line, but will not perform well when short casts are required and this will be very noticeable when fishing into a headwind. Soft rods are the reverse of this, they are great for short casts but not so good when you need a long cast in windy conditions. I personally prefer a rod that isn't too fast, which handles well for both short and long casting.

The second task required of a rod is something that is often ignored when considering which one to buy, and that is how effectively it will play fish. Bonefish are one of the hardest fighting fish the angler will encounter on a fly rod, so it is important to ensure that the rod has enough mid flex to cushion the demands placed on the rod and angler by the bonefish during the fight. This last point is important because some of the best casting rods are extremely stiff and whilst they will cast a long line they often have an unforgiving action that will be a handicap when playing a bonefish at close quarters.

The last point you need to consider is the durability of the rod? Saltwater rods have to be strong enough to cope with some serious and regular abuse. They will be dropped, immersed in saltwater from time to time, will have to endure the testing demands of very hard fighting fish, will occasionally have a lead-eyed fly whack into the top section when casting and also put up with the occasional clumsy guide who will try and ram your rod into the rod holes at the side of the skiff. All of these things will happen from time to time, so do make sure that your chosen rod is strong enough to cope. It is also important that the rods you use come with a no strings attached warranty, which can be called upon when needed.

Like rods, reels also need to be chosen with care and there are a number of superb reels specifically designed for saltwater fly fishing. For me the reel has to be of a strong design that is, once again, robust enough to stand up to the rigours of bonefishing year in and year out. A first-class drag is, not surprisingly, essential and I prefer reels with a large cork disk drag that I can maintain. At the end of each bonefishing trip I only need to apply a small amount of oil to the surface of the cork drag and the odd dab of grease to keep my reels in top condition.

One of the traits of a bonefish is its ability to swim towards the angler at speed, so a large arbour reel is required to keep up with the fish. I am also keen on reels that have the minimum number of holes in the back plate, or preferably none at all. Many of the latest fly reels designed for saltwater fly fishing do have holes in the back plate, or in some cases very little back plate whatsoever, which is just asking for sand to find its way into the inner workings of the reel. Not surprisingly, all my reels have a solid back plate with no holes and because of this I very

Bonefish Stuff

rarely have to remove grains of sand. The size of reel will obviously be linked to the line size, but should be capable of holding 200 yards of backing.

As a general rule you get what you pay for with reels and anyone contemplating going bonefishing on a regular basis will be well advised to invest in high-quality reels designed for saltwater fly fishing. In the long run they will provide many years of trouble-free service and prove a good investment.

Once a reel is purchased it needs to be loaded with around 200 yards of backing and a tropical fly line specifically designed for bonefishing. There is a variety of backing available in different materials and breaking strains. I always use 30lb Dacron because it is durable and has a large diameter, which I find more comfortable to work with than 20lb. I don't use gel spun backing because I find it too thin, especially in 20-pound breaking strain, and I worry that a small cut from a sharp piece of rock or coral would reduce its strength. Tangles in the backing also mysteriously occur from time to time and they are much easier to untangle with 30lb Dacron. The only downside with 30lb Dacron is that it can be difficult to get 200 yards on a typical bonefish-size large arbour reel and for this reason I use Tibor Riptides for all my bonefishing, as they will easily accommodate this amount of backing.

Excellent fly lines are now easy to come by and all the major manufacturers provide dedicated bonefish lines, but they do vary in their profile, colour and stiffness. The angler will have to consider which profile is best suited to their rod and casting style. As far as colour is concerned, I avoid bright and garish lines, preferring subdued colours that are less likely to scare fish. It's also worth considering the durability of the fly line; some lines do have a harder coating than others and this needs to be considered, especially if you are likely to encounter mangroves – a hooked bonefish running through mangroves at speed can do real damage to fly lines. It is for this reason that I prefer stiff bonefish lines as I find they last longer and cast better in tropical environments. This last point is important as a casting deck can get extremely hot and stiffer lines are better able to cope with high temperatures than soft ones.

Apart from the fly itself, the final item of tackle is the leader, which is an important link in the chain that connects the angler to the bonefish. If you get this bit wrong then you will be losing more bonefish than you should. My own golden rule when bonefishing is to use the fewest number of knots possible, and for this reason I always use 10-foot knotless leaders. This means that the only knots on the leader are the one that connects it to the fly line and the one that connects to the fly. Any other knot in the leader will be the critical point of weakness. There are 9-foot knotless leaders available, but the problem with them is that once they have been tied to the fly line and fly to the leader, the length will then be closer to 8 feet, which is too short. This length will be further reduced each time a fly is changed and it is for this reason I use the 10-foot leaders. Occasionally, a longer leader will be required, especially for tailing bonefish in very still conditions and in this instance I tie on an extra 3 or 4 feet of tippet, but only if it is absolutely necessary. The other important point about leaders is the strength and as bonefish are generally not line shy I use 13-pound monofilament leaders for virtually all my bonefishing. Very rarely do I need to go lower than this.

Along with the tapered leaders, I take spools of leader material and make sure that they are of the same make and material as the leader, as I feel that the knots will be stronger as result. A selection of breaking strains between 10 and 16 pounds will do for most bonefishing situations.

The next subject to consider when bonefishing is clothing. This is clearly an important aspect of the sport as spending a day on a bonefish flat, especially when wading, can be very demanding. This is, of course, hardly surprising when you consider that the angler will have to endure high temperatures, bright sunlight, strong winds, rain, salt water, sand and sharp rocks. Fortunately, there is vast selection of high-quality clothing available to make the bonefisher as protected, comfortable and fashionable as possible.

Shirts and trousers need to be light and, if possible, come with a sun factor rating of at least 30. I prefer long trousers rather that shorts as they protect the legs better and also remove the need to continually apply sun lotion to your legs. This also applies to shirts and I always use long sleeves for the same reason. I prefer shirts with fastened/button down collars because unfastened collars will continually flap against your neck during a high-speed skiff ride. This can be painful as I discovered during my first, hour-long ride to the West Side of Andros! I also like reasonably spacious chest pockets which are handy for small fly boxes.

Bonefish shirts now come in a wide range of colours and it is not uncommon to see anglers ready to embark on a day's fishing wearing yellow, orange and red shirts. It might just be possible to get away with wearing such bright colours when fishing only from a skiff and on a cloudy day, but I cannot help but think that such bright colours would be a disadvantage when wading for tailing bonefish on a bright day. It is for this reason I only ever wear shirts that are tan or a subdued shade of blue.

Because exposure to the sun has to be treated with care a lightweight, fast-drying cap with a long peak which is dark underneath is important. I usually use two caps throughout the day, a normal one that I use first thing in the morning or when it is cloudy and another with a flap that covers the neck. I use the flap version throughout the day when it is sunny. I also consider it essential to have a pair of sungloves, as they protect the hands and, once again, remove the need to continually apply sun lotion. When I do use sun lotion it is always waterproof factor 50 which does the trick but is almost impossible to wash off in the shower at the end of the day!

Bonefish Stuff

Of course, it won't always be sunny when fishing the flats and there will be times when it is both cold and wet, so a thoroughly waterproof Gore-Tex type wading jacket should be carried. I always wear my waterproof jacket whilst travelling in a skiff to and from the flats, as it can be pretty cold and when it is windy the ride can be very wet indeed. Another time a waterproof jacket will repay itself is during a heavy storm, especially when they last an hour or two and the air temperature really plummets.

The final items of clothing are flats boots and I take two types on most bonefish trips. The first are some very heavy duty boots that are capable of withstanding sharp objects. On some of the Bahamian limestone islands, such as Eleuthera or Andros which have some very rough rocky beaches, then heavy duty boots will be needed to give adequate protection to both feet and ankles. The other boots I use are lightweight neoprene slip-ons which are ideal for wading sand flats. They are comfortable to wear and you can get them on and off very quickly, which is especially useful when fishing from a skiff and the guide suddenly says you need to wade. With both set of boots I use thin, tan coloured socks which help protect feet from sand abrasion. The wear and tear that your feet will have to put up with over a week-long bonefishing trip is considerable, especially if there is a lot of wading, so it is well worth looking after them!

So, after kitting yourself out with the appropriate tackle and clothing you'll have to consider the myriad of other stuff that you need when bonefishing. Before I embark on any bonefishing trip I use checklist to remind me of all the items I need to take with me and whilst I don't want to go through each item here, there are some that are essential for any trip.

Top of the list will always be a good pair of Polaroid glasses and in fact I take two just in case I lose or break a pair, which I have done in the past. I also take a replacement pair of my prescription glasses for the same reason. You can get Polaroids with a number of different lens' colours and some are, reputedly, designed to work better in some light conditions than others, but I am happy just to stick with brown which works fine for me. What I do find handy is a strap for the glasses, so that they hang from my neck when I need remove them to tie on a fly or change a leader or unhook a fish; this ensures I don't lose them! It is also worth taking along a small pack of tissues to clean the lenses, as they will continually get splashed, especially during skiff rides – bonefish can at times be very difficult to see and you don't want to handicap yourself with dirty glasses!

Something else I wouldn't be without is the small pair of fishing pliers and holster that I attach to my belt. I find these invaluable for snipping line and pressing down the barb on flies. The fact they are readily available on my belt means I don't have to go hunting for them in pockets or bags. I also have a very small sharpening stone which inserts into the same holster and, once again, it is

Bonefish Stuff

there ready to hone the point of the fly when needed. I have often seen bonefisher's adorned with a lanyard full of snips, pliers, spools of line and so on but this is a recipe for snagging up the line and I like to be as uncluttered as possible when bonefishing.

An area where there has been a great advance in the last few years is around photography and there are now some excellent waterproof cameras available that are small and lightweight. These are ideal for bonefishing and perfect for wading as there is no need to worry about the camera getting wet – some of the waterproof cameras also take surprisingly high quality-shots.

I used to take along a tape measure to determine the length of a bonefish and work out the weight, as using weighing scales isn't really an option when bonefishing, but I have now marked my rods to show different measurements. I have found this a faster and more practical way to measure fish.

When wading I take all that I need in a small bum bag, or fanny pack as they are called in the US. Some of the latest versions are huge, more like a rucksack, and the thought of wading with one of them around my waist on a hot day doesn't bare thinking about. My own bum bag is just big enough to hold a fly box, a couple of leaders, some tippet spools, a camera and a small bottle of water and I have never had the need to add to this list. The bag doesn't weigh much and I can happily wade with it around my waist for hours.

Each angler is different and their list may contain items that I haven't mentioned, but what is important is that the bonefisher is comfortable fishing the flats and that they have the utmost confidence in the kit they use. These are the things we do have control over, unlike the fish and the weather, so it pays to spend some time and thought getting this bit right.

Chapter 13

Getting There

Stepping on to a skiff at the start of a week's bonefishing is likely to be the result of many hours of painstaking preparation as destinations, guides, accommodation, flights and much more are researched. And the effort put into this will be greater the further you live from your chosen destination. Having said that, I thoroughly enjoy putting in the effort because it is an integral and fun part of a bonefishing trip and if the preparation and planning is done well, the end result will be an enjoyable and productive bonefishing trip.

Nowadays, I prefer to book my own flights, accommodation and guides, but for anyone starting out I would recommend going with an organized trip to get a flavour of spending a week or so bonefishing and an understanding of what is required. There are a number of companies that specialize in organizing hosted saltwater fly fishing trips; I have used some of them at various times and they have all been very reliable. My usual destination is the Bahamas and the countries around the Caribbean, simply because I can get there in a single day from the UK. Destinations further out, such as those in the Indian Ocean or Pacific, will require two days' travelling time, there and back, which reduces the amount of available fishing time. During a typical week in the Bahamas I can leave the UK on a Saturday morning and arrive on my chosen out island the same day. I then have six full days' fishing and can be back home the following Sunday.

The actual destination is very much down to the angler's aspirations and interests, but it is important to do as much research as possible. Some destinations will be particularly suitable for someone new to bonefishing; Mexico is one such place where there are large numbers of small to medium-sized bonefish which will give the angler plenty of opportunities to cast to and catch, which is the only way to learn and hone skills. Other destinations, such as Andros, will offer the chance of much bigger bonefish and will suit the more experienced bonefisher. The internet is a fantastic tool to help select the right place to go and you can uncover many of the fine details needed to make an informed decision about choosing a bonefish destination. Other anglers are also a key source of information and can give details and opinions that might not be available on the internet. For this reason, I never miss an opportunity to quiz other bonefishers on places they have fished and what they caught there.

Once a destination has been chosen, but before booking any flights, hotels and guides, the next action should be to decide exactly when to go – my favourite time for bonefishing is November, with May or early June a close second. November has a lot going for it, as it is generally out of the hurricane season and the water temperatures are still high enough to see plenty of bonefish on the flats. Over the years I have found the weather more predictable in November than in May, with good periods of sunny weather and not too much rain. I also feel that that the average size of bonefish appears larger at this time of year so if big bonefish are your aim then November can be a very productive month.

Other factors that need to be taken into account when deciding when to plan a bonefish trip are tides and phases of the moon. Tides really are important and selecting a week when they are at their optimum height for your chosen destination and flats area will always reap rewards. As a general rule, I have found a week of low tides to be far more productive than a week of high tides. This is very much linked to where you are fishing and there will certainly be destinations or individual flats where the reverse is true and which will fish better on a high tide. Only your guide, with his local knowledge, will be able to answer this accurately and I find that a guide's ability to understand exactly how much water there will be over an individual flat at a given time is one of the main skills that differentiates a good guide from an excellent one. All the best guides I have fished with are very adept at this. If it's possible, it is always worth chatting to guides before you make any final arrangements to your trip to find out which tides work best. At destinations such as the Bights of Andros, high tides mean that the bonefish will be feeding well into the mangroves and there will be less fish out on the flats. It can be very frustrating sitting in a skiff on the edge of dense mangroves listening to feeding bonefish as they crash around in the interior! Conversely, in the Joulter Cays area of Andros, where there is little in the way of mangroves, high tides will see either large schools of very nervous bonefish that are in tight shoals or the fish will be in the deeper channels and away from the flats. Low tides therefore will have an opposite effect and the angler will have a much better chance at fishing for small groups or tailing singles, which is what we are all after. This is, of course, a generalization and tides do have a habit of throwing up surprises but, on the whole, I have found low tides offer more productive fishing.

I'm not so sure about the impact of the moon, although I am fully aware that there is a school of thought that says that a full moon is detrimental to fishing. The theory is that on a full moon bonefish supposedly feed at night. This may be the case, but I am not convinced that it has any real influence on daytime fishing, not least because I have had some really excellent fishing following a bright, full moon. However, I will try to get a week's fishing with as little moon as possible, just to be on the safe side and, of course, moon phases are linked to tide levels.

Getting There

Once the week of a bonefish trip has been decided, flights can arranged, and accommodation and guides booked. Flights and somewhere to stay are pretty straight forward but, of course, the quality of the rooms and food needs to be of a high standard. This doesn't mean that it needs to be expensive but rooms need to be clean and the food plentiful and tasty!

Picking the right guide is, as you would expect, extremely important. Thankfully, I have only fished with poor guides on a couple of occasions, but the experience was enough to convince me that you need to pay as much care and attention to selecting your guide as possible. The best way to achieve this is to do as much research as you can, and personal recommendation from other anglers is undoubtedly the best way to select a good guide. It is well worth remembering that an excellent guide will need to know where the bonefish will be at any given stage of the tide, be good at spotting fish in inclement weather, have a first-class skiff to fish from and be pleasant company. The other important point is that once you have found a good guide never lose their contact details!

Tipping guides is also important and my approach when fishing from a lodge is to ask about the expected tip. If I am with a guide just for one day then tipping will be done once the fishing is over, but on a week-long trip I tip the guide at the end of the week. I let them know I will be doing this just so they know that they will be getting a tip. Generally, tips are around 10% of the daily rate but on days that have been special for one reason or another, or a guide has done an exceptional job over the course of a week, I will increase the tip.

For a November trip I would normally aim to have everything booked by late summer which gives me plenty of time to start getting into the bonefish mood and going through all of my gear and making sure everything is as it should be, which is something I really enjoy. This will also be an opportunity for me to spend some time at the fly tying vice making sure I have enough flies and in the right sizes and weights. The amount of stuff needed for a bonefish trip is considerable and I have created a very detailed spreadsheet listing all the necessities. This guarantees that nothing is forgotten when I get round to the packing stage.

As anyone who flies regularly knows, a long-haul trip on a plane is not what used to be. When I first started bonefishing I could carry my cherished rods and reels on to the plane and store them in the overhead luggage compartment, but not anymore. Pretty much everything needs to go in the hold, and for this reason it is essential to have just one bag for all of your kit and this includes rods. I still see anglers wrestling with large rod tubes at airports, but in this day and age, with so many excellent four-piece rods available, it is unnecessary as all your equipment can go in one bag. My own bag is a large holdall, 33 inches in length, which can accommodate four fly rods, a spinning rod plus all the associated reels, tackle and clothing.

Getting There

The clothing is especially important as it will help cushion expensive items of equipment from the rigours of airport baggage handlers and machinery.

All major airlines stipulate a baggage allowance which is normally around 42 pounds or 20 kilograms. On a week-long trip I will test this limit to the full, especially if I have to take along my heavy duty wading boots. Because of this, it is important to take into consideration how much your holdall weighs. I am mystified by the weight of some of the bags aimed at anglers; it is not uncommon to see bags advertised by some fishing tackle outfitters that can weigh in excess of 12 pounds, which is over a quarter of the baggage allowance! My own bag weighs in at a fraction over 3 pounds which means I can carry more gear if needed. The bag also has wheels which I find are essential as there is often a fair amount of walking to do around airports, especially between terminals if you have a connecting flight. You don't want to put your back out at the start of a bonefishing trip!

Something else that I do to help keep the weight down when travelling is to transport my rods in light, rigid, plastic tubes instead of the very pretty but heavy metal tubes they are stored in at home. It is possible to get two fly rods into one 3-inch diameter plastic tube. In order to do this the two rods will need to go in the plastic tube with the rod handles at opposite ends or they won't fit. The plastic tubes will keep your rods safe from breakage but with much less weight.

A Bonefishing Journey

The one other area I pay particular attention to when considering what to take is spare items of tackle and on a number occasions I've been very glad I packed extra equipment. The most obvious item is an additional rod, as I have had a number break over the years, usually as a result of a fly hitting the top section at speed on a very windy day, or a rod being clumsily stored in a rod compartment on the side of the skiff. The rod doesn't break straight away, but the tip section usually goes a day a two later. Because of this I always carry a spare 8 weight rod, which is the weight of rod I use most of the time when bonefishing. I also take along a spare reel complete with line, just in case.

As I mentioned at the beginning of this chapter, I view the preparation stage and all that it involves as very much part of the trip. It certainly helps to feed the eager anticipation that slowly builds as the trip approaches.

For the journey home, which always comes around far too soon, I follow the same routine, but in reverse. The only difference is that pretty much all of the tackle and bonefish clothing now has a saltwater sheen, despite the fact it may have been hosed down at the end of every fishing day. When I am back home one of my first jobs is to fill the bath with cold water and soak those items of tackle that have been subjected to salt water. This will include rods, reels, pliers and also my boots and any bags that were taken on the skiff, as they would have had a good soaking. Once everything has been thoroughly rinsed, I put rods and reels in a warm place to dry out and then carry out any necessary maintenance, which is usually just some oil and grease on reels. When all this is done, everything can be packed safely away and I am ready to start researching the next bonefishing trip!

Chapter 14

Tactics

Although it does matter what rods, reels, lines and flies you use it is, ultimately, the angler's skill and awareness that makes the biggest difference between a very successful bonefishing day and an average one. I have mentioned before that there are some excellent books written about bonefishing and I am not going to replicate here all of the tips and guidance on how to catch bonefish. However, I do want to focus on a small number of things that have certainly helped me to catch more bonefish and turned potentially average days into memorable ones.

As we all know, the bonefisher will encounter many things in a day's fishing that are out of their control, such as the weather, tides and the availability and mood of the bonefish. There isn't much we can do about any of these factors and without this unpredictable aspect, bonefishing would be very dull. There are, however, some things the angler can control and taking time to prepare for the day's fishing is one of them. For me this will include making sure that all of my tackle is set up correctly and that leaders and knots are as they should be. I always tie on fresh leaders and flies before the day begins; tapered leaders cost very little, especially when compared to the overall cost of a day's bonefishing, and it is worth making this extra small investment. Flies are tied on using a non-slip mono loop knot which I find imparts extra movement into the fly. It is also important to make sure that the fly is really sharp and I continually check this throughout the fishing day, and immediately after catching a fish, as the point can often be turned over slightly because of the bonefish's hard mouth. There will also be many items of tackle, clothing and sundry items that need to be checked and this should be done beforehand. You only have to forget wading boots, sun lotion or a box of flies to really ruin a day, so a few moments making sure that you have all you need is essential and time well spent.

The next key area is your ability to cast. The folly of paying out good money for a bonefishing trip and then wasting it because of an inability to cast is often highlighted in magazines and books. I fully endorse this and to be consistently successful at bonefishing requires the ability to cast well in all weather conditions. It would be great if the right-handed caster had a continual left to right breeze as it would be easy to lay out a long line every time, but in reality this is far from the case. Strong winds from every direction will form an integral part of bonefishing. The ability to cast accurately and in all weather conditions is one of the most important skills the bonefisher needs. One way to do this is to learn how to cast with both the right and left hands or, as I do, be able to cast in a left-handed manner but using the right hand. This is achieved by the right-handed caster bringing the back cast across their left shoulder instead of the more conventional right shoulder and with practice this is an easy and effective way to deal with strong winds from the wrong direction. This also works equally well for the left hander where, of course, everything is done in reverse. Whatever style you adopt the ability to cast effectively, regardless of the wind direction will prove invaluable. I would advise anyone who is about to embark on a bonefishing trip for the first time to consider having casting lessons or, at the very least, spending some time practicing casting, especially into the wind.

The other area of casting that I find difficult, and I am sure that I share this challenge with many other bonefishers, is casting directly into a very strong headwind. Guides are very good at this and do not need much persuasion to demonstrate their casting prowess, but you will find that when they return the rod to you the leader is likely to be full of wind knots! Therefore, casting effectively into the wind, making sure that the fly turns over and without creating wind knots is difficult for everyone, but there are some things that have worked for me. The first is to use a short leader of no more than 7 or 8 feet. When it is very windy bonefish often lose their inhibitions and will not be so aware of the fly line so a short leader is no handicap.

Tactics

The second tactic is to use a heavier fly and, instead of using a medium bead chain, I use a fly with lead eyes which really cuts through the wind and helps turn over the fly. Once again, the strong wind and associated waves will cushion the impact of the fly and the bonefish won't be spooked by this. In fact, on a very windy day they often seem to be attracted to the plop of the heavier fly and it is not uncommon to see them turn in the direction of where the fly has landed and zoom over and take it! Despite the challenges of casting in very windy weather, I relish the opportunity as bonefish are more aggressive when there are heavy waves about. Some of my most memorable fishing has been under such conditions.

Of course, it's no good being proficient at casting if you cannot see the fish – the ability to spot bonefish is probably the most important skill a bonefisher can possess. It is relatively easy to do this at midday with a bright sun in a cloudless blue sky and little wind, but as we know these days can be all too rare. More often than not it will be windy and cloudy and this is when the ability to spot fish makes the difference between a good and bad day. If you are fishing with a good guide then much of the work will be done for you but, if like me, you prefer wading on your own, which gives me a greater sense of achievement when I catch a bonefish, then you will need to know what to look for. It is also worth remembering that when fishing from a skiff you are in an elevated position, quite high above the water, and this makes fish spotting easier. When wading, you will be much lower and, as a consequence, spotting fish will be that much harder.

When I first started bonefishing I would scan the water no more than perhaps 30 or 40 yards out, but nowadays I look out and scan the water before me right out to the horizon. It's amazing what you can pick up and over time you will develop an almost sixth sense around spotting bonefish. On windy days the secret will be to look for changes in wave patterns, and this can vary from an almost imperceptible change in the uniformity of the waves right through to big areas of nervous water created by large groups of bonefish. This last phenomenon is usually referred to as a push. On still days it may be just a glint from the tail of a bonefish or the merest ripple where one shouldn't be. The important thing is to focus on anything you see that shouldn't be there!

The actual fishing strategy you employ will need to fit whatever water disturbance you have before you. For example, a small disturbance may be from one or two slow moving fish and after wading or poling in their general direction I would expect to spot and cast to an individual fish. A fast moving push of nervous water will need a cast that is directed well in front of the area of disturbed water; if you cast into the nervous water you will be casting at the tail of the school and are unlikely to be successful.

Another indication of the presence of bonefish is cloudy water and by this I am not referring to a mud. When I first started bonefishing my guides would often look around

Tactics

the skiff and say that bonefish have been feeding in the area. At the time I thought they knew this because they could see signs of feeding on the bottom, but I soon came to realize that, when just one or two bonefish feed, they create a very slight cloudiness in water and this is what you should look out for. Sometimes it is barely perceptible, but if you do detect it then usually a fish will soon come into view and on cloudy days when your view will be reduced, this cloudy water is a very helpful indicator of the presence of bonefish.

Once you have spotted your fish you have to decide how to actually fish for them and this will depend on what the bonefish are doing at the time. This activity will be closely linked to the various stages of the tide and the habitat being fished as there are a number of bonefish formations and behaviours that can be encountered.

On even, light sandy flats at high tide it is common to see large, tightly packed schools of bonefish that may contain many hundreds of fish. Usually, these schools will move slowly across a flat and a fly cast just in front of the group will prove successful. As the tide recedes, then a school will start to disperse into small groups of fish which gives the angler the opportunity to select and fish for larger bonefish they may choose to target. Once again, a fly cast just ahead of a small moving group will work. The final stage is often at low tide in very skinny water when the bonefish break into ones and twos and start tailing and for me this is the very pinnacle of the sport. The opportunity to cast to and catch tailing bonefish will give the angler some cherished moments.

I think that fishing for tailers is very different from the approach normally taken, because the fish can be ultra-sensitive to noise and movement, so everything the angler does needs to be stealthy. Wading needs to be slow and delicate, casting needs to be done with the minimum number of false casts and be accurate first time. Finally, the leader needs to be long enough to drop what is often an unweighted fly in the right spot, without spooking the fish. When casting to tailing bonefish I use the same technique that I use for casting a dry fly on rivers for brown trout, which is to cast at a spot 3 feet above where you intend the fly to land. This will ensure that the fly lands as quietly as possible. A cast aimed directly at the surface is likely to result in the fly being slapped into the surface which simply doesn't work on tailers.

The other challenge with tailing bonefish is that they are so focused on feeding that they will rarely see a fly that is cast more than 3 or 4 feet away from them, so the ability to accurately cast to within a foot or two is paramount. There is, of course, always the risk that if you cast the fly closer than this you will almost certainly spook the bonefish, so there is a fine line between success and failure. The only exception is when the bonefish upends and really gets its head down on a food item they have spotted. When they do this, if you are quick enough, you can cast right on top of them without them knowing and then move the fly when they return to an even keel. Providing your fly is at the head end of the bonefish, rather than the tail, they normally pounce on the fly with real aggression and the fun really begins!

Fly construction is often quite critical when fishing for tailing bonefish as the fly needs to enter the water quietly so that it doesn't spook the fish. I either use a fly with light bead chain eyes or none at all. As tailing bonefish will generally be in very shallow water then any fly with heavier eyes will generate too much of a "plop" as it lands. I like flies with legs for tailers as this helps to soften the impact. Tying in a palmered hackle is also good for quietening down the entry of the fly and I use this on some patterns. Tailing bonefish will often be found over turtle grass and for this reason it is vital for the fly to have a weed guard as there is nothing worse than casting in exactly the right spot only for the fly to snag on weed when it is retrieved. One word of caution – shop bought flies often have mono weed guards that are far too stiff and will prevent a proper hook up, so I always tie in my weed guards using 20lb hard nylon which I have found avoids weed, but still allows an effective hook up. As a general rule when fishing for tailers, I have found that it is the construction of the fly that is probably more important than the pattern.

When wading, rather than fishing from a skiff, then the strategy you adopt is very important. There will be times when it is better to wade across a flat in search of bonefish and there will be other times when it pays to stay put and let them come to you. As a rule, if there is a strong flow from the tide, then I have found it best to stand in a spot I think the bonefish will be moving through, and on most flats there are one or two places where this occurs. If you can find the right place it is possible to stay there for perhaps an hour and regularly catch bonefish as they swim towards you. This is likely to continue until the tide changes and alters the behaviour of the bonefish, and I have had some large catches of bonefish when fishing in this way.

The other strategy is to wade across a flat, and the ideal time to do this is at low tide when the bonefish will have spread out over the flat and be feeding, either as singles or in small pods. At times like this I very slowly and quietly make my way across the flat, looking for tailers and nervous water and target fish whenever I find them. One other time I wade is when there isn't much going on and I wade quite quickly trying to cover as much of the flat as possible. Sometimes you will find bonefish localized in just one area of the flat, so it pays to cover a flat in this way until you find them.

One aspect of bonefishing where I often find myself disagreeing with guides is how to retrieve the fly. The common instruction will be "strip strip" and whilst really hungry and aggressive bonefish will take the fly that is stripped in this fashion, a more cautious bonefish, especially a big one, probably won't. My preferred method is to move the fly until the bonefish has seen it and then leave it stationary for the bonefish to pick it up. Generally speaking, once a bonefish has seen the fly and is following it, they will nearly always pick it up. If you keep stripping then you are just as likely to pull the fly out of the bonefish's mouth just as it is about to take it. If you do employ this strip stop technique, then your guide is likely to be shouting at you to keep stripping the fly, but you need to hold your nerve and leave the fly where it is – it usually pays off in the end!

The other type of take that I get more and more is from a completely stationary fly. I stumbled upon this many years ago in Los Roques when I had a vicious take on a small crab pattern I had cast out and then left to rest on the bottom. I have used this technique many times over the years and found it very effective on wary bonefish that are heavily fished. On some flats that see a lot of bonefishers I will only fish a stationary fly. It also works well when casting into a big school of fish and a stationary fly will often result in a firm take if it is left to lie on the bottom for a short while.

I think most bonefishers are familiar with the strip strike technique for setting the hook and it really is the only way. The key to successful hook ups is to make sure the rod is pointing directly at the fish and to keep stripping once you are certain the bonefish has taken the fly. The only time I don't do this is when I am fishing from a skiff and get a take that is so close to the boat that it is impossible to point the rod at the fish and perform an effective strip strike. When this happens I get in two or three very quick upward strikes which usually sets the hook. You have to be careful though, because if you put in one strike too many just as the bonefish is heading off in the opposite direction there will only be one outcome, and it won't be the one you are looking for!

Once hooked, the bonefish will give the angler, pound for pound, one of the most exciting fights they will ever experience, as a fit, ocean side bonefish of 7 or 8 pounds can really deliver a turn of speed. My approach to playing bonefish is to get them in as quickly as possible, so that they still have enough energy to swim off strongly when released. For this reason I use 13-pound leaders, although I will go up to 16 pounds if I am likely to encounter big bonefish, and I have the drag on the reel set as tight as possible without risking breaking the line. I have seen anglers try and alter the drag by using their fingers to control the tension of the spool but this is not ideal as is likely to result in either a break off or overrun. My advice would be to purchase a very high-quality saltwater fly reel with a first-class drag and let the reel do all the work.

As I have already said many times, bonefishing is fascinating and addictive and it is the need to continually change your fishing strategy that makes it so appealing. In the course of a typical day the temperature will change, the tides will ebb and flow and the behaviour of the bonefish will respond to each and every change. The angler, in turn, needs to be aware of the changes that will

Tactics

be happening on a flat, some obvious and others less so, and use them to their advantage – bonefishing is a fascinating business and it is the need to continually evaluate your game plan that makes it so.

Chapter 15

Gotcha

My original intention was to write a chapter on bonefish flies, but then I realized that the vast majority of bonefish I now catch come to just one fly – the Gotcha. So this chapter will be devoted to the Gotcha and I will cover the very small selection of other flies I sometimes need to use in a separate chapter.

To say that I use one fly for most of the time is somewhat misleading, it would be far more accurate to say that I use just one pattern and that pattern, the Gotcha, is available in many different guises in both size and weight. I believe that the most important thing about a bonefish fly is that it should be of the correct size and weight to fish effectively and that these two factors are of the upmost importance. Although the type of fly used is the main consideration, I believe that size and weight take precedence over the actual pattern. Having said that, there will be times when the choice of pattern becomes quite critical, but I have found these occasions to be isolated and very much a rarity.

Gotcha

One of the advantages of focusing on just one pattern is that it takes one important variable out of the equation, which is fly selection, and this enables the angler to concentrate on other important aspects of catching bonefish. As I said, the size and weight of the fly are both crucial to success. Looking through my own box of Gotchas shows that I have them in four different sizes and five different weights, and in total there are eight different permutations of fly. This means I can cover all depths, weather conditions and bonefish feeding patterns that I am likely to encounter with just this one pattern.

It's very easy to imagine that bonefishing is all about standing shin deep in warm water, with a gentle breeze under a cloudless blue sky and schools of tailing bonefish drifting into view, eager to take your fly. This does of course happen and you can, on occasion, experience the fishing of a lifetime, but there will be other days when you won't see a sign of a bonefish or, more frustratingly, that the fish are there but are not taking your fly. It is this last scenario that is the most challenging and if you are fishing with a guide and have had several fish either ignore your fly, or refuse it, then it will only be a matter of time before your guide will ask you to put on a Gotcha.

The Gotcha now seems to have taken over from the Crazy Charlie as the number one universal bonefish fly, and it doesn't seem to matter whether you are fishing the creeks in Cayo Largo or the endless flats in the Bahamas, it will work equally well. If you look closely at a Gotcha it is easy to see why the fly is so effective, especially when you watch how it behaves in the water. The combination of the not too shiny body and tail materials, coupled with the translucent quality of the craft fur wing, really does mimic the see-through characteristics of the shrimps that inhabit bonefish flats and make up such a large proportion of the bonefish diet. What's more, tying a Gotcha is quick and relatively simple, which is important when you consider how hard saltwater fishing is on flies and that, on an average trip, you may be spending quite some time at the vice! If you are planning a bonefishing trip then you could do worse than to spend some time at the vice before you get on the plane, tying up some Gotchas in a variety of sizes and weights. The fly is easy to tie, but you do need to pay attention to detail to get it just right.

When tying any bonefish fly it is essential to make sure you use hooks that are proven to be reliable; it is amazing what a 3-pound bonefish can do to a hook, so they must be strong. The hook pattern I use most often, and have found consistently reliable, is the Tiemco 811S which is very strong and stays sharp. It is also easy to de-barb, the barb will neatly break off when pressed with small pliers. Although most bonefish patterns will call for a size 4 hook, the destination you are going to fish will dictate what size of fly you should tie. For example, when on a trip to Eleuthera, in the Bahamas, I use flies only in size 6 and 8 as the bonefish are nervous of any fly tied on a size 4. Conversely, when fishing the West Side of Andros,

Gotcha

I use Gotchas 4 inches long tied on a size 2 for most of the time! The golden rule is to go small for nervous fish and use larger hooks for big, aggressive bonefish, as is the case at Andros.

Tying a Gotcha, as with most bonefish flies, starts with the eyes which are essential if the fly is to fish upside down and in the proper manner. Generally they will be medium silver bead chain but you can go up or down a bead size depending on the depth of water. On flats, where the water is around mid-calf deep, then medium bead chain will be fine, but for water that is knee-deep I use large bead chain eyes, especially if fishing from a skiff. It is important that the fly gets down to the bottom in about 3 seconds which is what you want to achieve to stay in control of the fly and keep an eye on the incoming fish. Occasionally, I will fish a very deep flat which may have a couple of feet of water over it and this will call for lead eyes to get the fly down.

For very skinny water, around ankle depth, which is often best for bonefish, you should still use eyes, but they need to be very small and give just enough weight to keep the fly fishing upright and on an even keel. Blind flies with no eyes at all are popular, but the fly will have a tendency to lean over to one side when retrieved and bonefish will often follow but reject a fly presented in this way. If you can use eyes, you should do so, but use the lightest you can get away with to avoid spooking the bonefish and making them more nervous than they are naturally.

The eyes should be placed on top of the hook shank, about 3mm from the eye in the case of a size 4 hook. This will leave enough room to tie in all of the materials behind the eye and produce a neat, well-balanced fly. When tying on the bead chain eyes I use strong pink, flat, waxed nylon thread and, once tied on, I superglue them in place a couple of times. I do this in batches of a dozen hooks at a time, which gives the glue plenty of time to set. It is important that they are securely glued on and do not move, to ensure that the fly sits perfectly upright, and fishes correctly.

Once the eyes are firmly in place then the pearl Mylar tail can be tied in. This should be at least the same length as the body and in the finished fly it will be flared out, but do not do this at this stage as it will just get in the way. When the tail is securely in place then tie in the pearl diamond braid body, but make sure this goes over a good layer of pink thread, which will assist the translucent appearance of the fly. Do not overlap the braid as the pink under body will not show through and it is important that the edges of the braid just butt up against each other when wound on. The diamond braid should be finished off by winding between the bead chain eyes in a figure of eight fashion and tied off in front of them.

When tying really big Gotchas on size 2 hooks or bigger I cover the diamond braid body with clear vinyl rib, which gives the fly some added bulk, and the fish seem to prefer it this way. I also keep the tail extra long.

Gotcha

The trickiest part of tying a Gotcha is the blond craft fur wing. Craft fur is used to make cuddly toys, amongst other things, and has both long hairs and a dense under fur. Genuine craft fur is becoming increasingly difficult to find so Polar Hair in shrimp colour is a good substitute. Only the long hairs need to be used, but I find it best to cut the craft fur at its base and then pull out the under fur leaving just the longer hair. Do not throw away the under fur as it makes excellent dubbing material for nymphs and dry flies! All the longer hairs are of different lengths so they will need to be rearranged so that the wing is reasonably dense, but it is important not to have the wing so thick that the shine of the body does not show through. Try not to have all the hairs the same length as this makes the fly look unnatural. The correct length of the wing should be just beyond the end of the tail, although when fishing for really big bones I use a wing that is up to four inches in length and a big bonefish will have no problem either seeing or inhaling the fly!

The final part of tying the Gotcha is to add just a few strands of crystal flash on top of the wing, but remember that in bright, sunny conditions this can really stand out and frighten bonefish, so it is best to use no more than 6 strands. Once these are in place and the head is finished, I put on a generous amount of varnish and let some of this soak into the base of the wing to make it really secure. You can also tease out the tail at this stage, with a dubbing needle, so that it flares out and the fly will be complete.

My standard Gotcha is tied with a blond wing with pearl crystal flash and I find this an excellent combination over hard, white sand. However, anyone new to bonefishing will quickly come to realize that there are many different types and colours of bottom. One of the most productive is soft marl, which bonefish really like as these are very rich food areas and it is easy for the fish to dig their noses into the soft sand and mud to root out food. The marl flats will be slightly darker than the hard sandy areas and here I find that a Gotcha with a tan craft fur wing works better than the standard version. I also use rainbow crystal flash on the big Gotchas as I want the fish to see the fly.

Actually fishing the Gotcha is much the same as with any other bonefish fly in that you will have to see what the bonefish want on the day! Sometimes they will want the fly retrieved on a strip stop basis but there will be many times when they will only pick up a stationary fly, and on these occasions it is best to stop stripping as soon as you are aware that the fish has seen the fly and strip strike when you see the fish pick up. This last technique is particularly useful when fishing for bonefish that are wary and see a lot of anglers.

Another important aspect to fishing the Gotcha is how it is tied on and there really is only one knot that can be used which is the non-slip mono loop. This allows the fly to move freely and it will fish perfectly upright whether it is moving or stationary. Any knot that is tight up against the eye of the fly such as a half turn blood knot or

Gotcha

grinner will constrict its free movement and the fly will have a tendency to lay flat when it is retrieved which is a definitely counterproductive when bonefishing. The non-slip mono loop can be a little tricky to tie neatly at first and this is especially the case if you have a school of feeding bonefish in front of you and your fingers are shaking! So it pays to practice the knot beforehand until you can tie it well every time under pressure.

The Gotcha is, of course, just one of many hundreds of different bonefish flies, and on any bonefish trip you will need to take a selection of other patterns to cater for the variety of different fishing situations that will be encountered, but the fly, as I have mentioned, has proven to be a real winner. If you are considering going bonefishing, and it doesn't really matter where, then do make sure you take some Gotchas along. It didn't get its name for nothing!

Chapter 16

Other Flies

I remember my formative days as a trout fisherman, when I read everything about trout fly fishing I could lay my hands on and, as a consequence, had so many boxes filled with flies I could hardly carry them all. Over time, of course, things changed and nowadays I use just a small selection of trout flies that I have perfected over the years and built up confidence in. I know that this frugal, practical approach catches me more trout, not less.

So, you would have expected that, having learnt this salutary lesson as a trout fisherman, I wouldn't have followed the same path as a novice bonefisherman. But of course I did not and, if truth be told, I enjoyed buying new flies and making others and would gaze lovingly at box after box of exotic and imaginatively named flies that their inventors had assured the angling world would do the business.

Of course I soon learnt, or to be more precise re-learnt, that this approach just doesn't work; not least because when you are standing on a bonefish flat, how do you

Other Flies

decide what fly to use out of the many hundreds of bright and colourful creations at your disposal? Furthermore, I soon came to realize that the size of a fly and its weight are equally important as the pattern, so how could I possibly carry so many flies in all the necessary size and weight permutations? It just wouldn't work. So, as with trout fishing, the light finally went on and I started to cull my fly collection to just a small selection of flies that I knew would work in all of the fishing conditions and habitats I was likely to encounter. It also meant that because I now had a manageable number of flies to work with I could carry each pattern in the variety of sizes and weights that is so crucial to success.

Having said all of this there was, of course, no short cut to finding this small selection of top flies. It was only by tying or buying this vast selection of flies and then using them that it became possible for me to hone them down to my ultimate choice and I guess this must have taken me at least six years.

As we all know, the end product of any fly should be to enable the angler to catch a bonefish and my approach to refining my ultimate fly selection was to look at what the fly has to achieve in order to consistently catch fish. Eventually I settled on four areas which were the colour, shape, size and the fly's ability to fish at the correct depth. Size is easy to address and my flies are generally tied on size 2, 4 and 6 hooks, which cover most situations. Only rarely will I tie up flies on a size 8 for very spooky bonefish. The ability to fish at the correct depth is down to how the fly is weighted and the patterns I use will be tied using small, medium and large bead chain and three different weights of lead dumbbell eyes. This range enables me to effectively fish skinny water right though to 6-foot deep flats or channels when required. The two aspects of the fly that need the most thought are the colour and shape, which are linked to the colour of the bottom be fished and the likely prey items the bonefish may be feeding on and my final selection of flies addresses both. So, what are the flies?

I mentioned earlier that the fly I use most is the Gotcha as it is a good shrimp representation. It is ideal for light coloured bottoms that the bonefisher is likely to encounter more than any other, but there will be other colours of bottom which dictate an alternative fly selection. The first of these is the brown, soft marl that is often encountered in creeks. I remember fishing the north tip of Andros where a mangrove-lined creek meanders for some way into the island. This creek has a famous landmark – a crashed plane that lies forlornly at the entrance of the creek. The story goes that the plane was carrying lobsters to Nassau, but crashed shortly after take-off; apparently the pilot escaped unharmed, but I'm not so sure about the fate of the lobsters! Anyone who has fished this creek will remember it well, as the site of the crashed plane is not easily forgotten.

On the day in question I started fishing over a typical white sandy bottom and had already caught some fish on

Other Flies

a Gotcha. We then moved into the creek and although there were bonefish around they just wouldn't take the Gotcha as it looked unnatural against the dark brown bottom. When I put on a big Borski Shrimp the effect was immediate. My first cast with it was way off target, landing about 12 feet away from the bonefish, but it didn't matter and the fish shot over towards it and grabbed it first time. I then had several more on the fly until the ebbing tide forced us out of the creek. I believe the fly worked well for two reasons: firstly it was exactly the same colour as the bottom and secondly, the dark bands on the fly mimicked the small baitfish in the creek that had similar bands. The Borski Shrimp always has a place in my fly box, as it is the right colour for darkish bottoms and is a chunky fly that really does imitate prey items. It also works well when tied with no eyes and a weed guard and it is very effective when fishing for tailers.

The other flat type that I fish a lot, and which requires careful fly selection, are those covered in turtle grass and, once again, the Gotcha is too bright a fly to work well amongst the vivid green of the grass flat. I always feel that small crabs are likely to be a staple food item in this habitat, so I like to use a fly with legs. The fly I have found particularly effective here is the Bonefish Bitters which can best be described as a generic crab pattern. The fly is, unquestionable, an imitative pattern and the bushy centre and legs are a good representation of a crab. The other thing about the Bonefish Bitters is that you can tie it or buy it in a variety of colours and this enables you to "match the hatch" so to speak and select a colour that resembles the colour of crab you are likely to encounter on the flat you are fishing.

I mostly use the Bonefish Bitters in orange as it seems to work best for me, and this colour is generally my first choice. The fly is particularly effective on the turtle grass flats in Cuba, especially in Cayo Largo, and is generally taken as soon as a bonefish sees it. When bonefish see a crab, or in this case a crab pattern, they don't stand on ceremony and really do attack the fly, so expect an aggressive take from the bonefish. Strip striking needs to be timed just right, if you hang on to the line too long your leader is likely to be broken, so I make sure I do a very short, sharp, strip strike and then let go of the line! Fishing with the Bonefish Bitters can be great fun in turtle grass but make sure you tie in a weed guard or you will be constantly hooking into weed.

The Bonefish Bitters also works well on light-coloured flats and I have found the tan coloured version works best here. As the fly looks like a prey item, then it is particularly effective when fished stationary and bonefish will happily take it this way.

My next fly is one I have founded particularly useful when fishing from sandy beaches on ocean side flats. These areas are often deep when compared to a more typical bonefish flat and, as the bottom can sometimes vary in colour, I have found that a Clouser Minnow,

Other Flies

especially a big size two, works very well. This is especially so in Los Roques where there is lot of beach fishing. The Clouser Minnow is a great all round fly and is always in my fly box. Not only does it work well when fished along the bottom but it is also an effective fry imitation and can be stripped back in mid-water. At Los Roques, the bonefish often feed on the glass minnow shoals and a white and green Clouser striped very quickly just a foot or so below the surface is readily attacked by the bonefish. Watch out for the takes though, as they can be very aggressive, requiring a strong leader. A chartreuse Clouser is also very effective on conventional flats, and when tied on a size four hook and with bead chain eyes comes very close to the Gotcha as a consistently effective bonefish fly.

I still do, of course, take several fly boxes containing many different patterns on each fishing trip, but they are only there "just in case", and for most of the time they will stay in their boxes. The vast majority of bonefish I catch will be on the Gotcha, with the remainder being caught on a Borski Shrimp, Clouser Minnow and Bonefish Bitters. Only when these flies fail to work will I start to look for alternatives.

Something I do feel really benefits the bonefisher is tying your own flies and all of the four main patterns I use most, I tie myself. This gives me complete control over the materials used and the way the fly is constructed in terms of its weight, size and durability. Perhaps the most important aspect of tying my own flies is that I have complete faith in them and this builds confidence, which is so important when bonefishing.

The selection of flies you use will reflect your own experience and also the destinations that are fished. One person's fly selection will be different from anothers. Whatever flies are ultimately chosen, and remember that this selection may change over time as some flies will be replaced with others, I do feel that the principal of using just a small selection of flies is a sound one. It gives the bonefisher the chance to become familiar with how to fish effectively with certain patterns and, as I have already said, it takes away the dilemma you face when having to choose a fly from a much larger selection. This allows the bonefisher to concentrate fully on fishing strategy.

Chapter 17

Boats

On the west side of Andros, when the tide isn't running, fishing from a skiff can be captivating. The bonefish, and they are normally good-sized ones, will be moving in singles or sometimes doubles and be feeding within just a few feet from the shore. At times like this the whole boat fishes as one, with the guide and the non-fishing angler and the angler up on the casting area, all intently looking for a sighting of a bonefish, which previous experience tells you, will surely come soon. When a bonefish is spotted the teamwork really begins. The guide will start to position the boat and the non-fishing angler, if there are three of you in the boat, will make sure there is nothing for the line to catch on when the cast is made. Fishing seems to really slow down at times like this, and there is almost too much time to think about where exactly you should cast to and when. Cast too early and you'll have to cast again which may spook the fish. Cast too late and the fish will sense you casting with the same end result, so timing and accuracy are crucial. Assuming that everything goes to plan, there is every chance the bonefish will be caught, and there will be handshakes all round in the boat at what was undoubtedly, a team effort.

Some bonefish destinations will require little in the way of actually fishing from a skiff and in places like Los Roques, Joulter Cays and the Ascension Bay area of Mexico, the boat will mainly be used to ferry the angler from one flat to another. However, there are other destinations where fishing from a skiff is an integral part of bonefishing and there are other places, such as the West Side and Bights of Andros, where there is little opportunity to fish in any other way. Fishing afloat like this can be very enjoyable and rewarding, but it must be approached in the correct way.

First and foremost you need a good guide with a clean, well-maintained skiff. I remember one late afternoon whilst fishing in Cuba when the skiff ran out of petrol, only to discover that the guide did not have a radio that worked, or any sort of flashlight or torch. Fortunately, I do carry a torch and this enabled our rescue boat to find us several hours later when it was dark. That salutary lesson immediately made me more vigilant about selecting the right boat and guide. Once again, research and homework will pay dividends here, and when fishing with a new guide for the first time you should give the boat a thorough visual check before you set out. If anything looks out of place or not quite up to what you are expecting, quiz the guide until your concerns are addressed.

Boats

When booking a day's bonefishing the angler will have the choice of either fishing alone, with just the guide, or sharing the boat with another angler. Splitting the cost of a boat is an obvious advantage here and it is nice to be able to share captures and memories with another angler. However, when fishing with someone else in a shared boat it is important that both anglers work together as a team and follow basic guidelines if angling harmony is to be maintained!

It helps if both anglers have a similar standard of angling ability. This will make life easier for the guide and also mean that, as each angler will be taking turns up front on the skiff, there will be a constant rotation between the two bonefishers. If one angler is a far more experienced bonefisher than the other they are likely to catch a fish at the first or second shot and then spend ages watching the other angler fluff chances which is frustrating for everyone in the boat who isn't fishing.

My regular boat partner is Trevor, we have fished together over many years and know how to work effectively as a team. The system we use to make sure we both have equal opportunities to catch bonefish is to take 30-minute turns to fish up front – that is until one of us catches a bonefish and then we will change over as soon as that happens. If we are at a destination where the fishing is mostly from the skiff, then we will catch an almost identical number of bonefish over a week's fishing which suggests it's a good system that is fair to both anglers.

One of the other key elements when fishing from a skiff is tidiness. There is nothing worse than having bags, coats and boots strewn over the well of the boat waiting for the line to catch on to just as the bonefish makes its first run – and this does happen! It is normally best for each angler to select one side of the boat and then store all their rods, bags and jackets on that same side – life is an awful lot easier this way. Sometimes guides will take both anglers rods, en masse, and stow them away on both sides of the boat so that they get jumbled up. When this happens I always take the time to rearrange them before setting off, so that my own rods are all on the same side of the boat – your guide will not mind.

Once everything is in place and the chosen flat has been found then the fishing can begin. It is worth remembering that 50 feet at 11 o'clock will not be exactly the same place for every guide, so before the fishing starts I will ask the guide to select a distance and clock position. I will then cast there just to make sure we are synchronized and if not, I will make the necessary adjustments to future casts. It is also worth doing a very long practice cast or two to get you prepared for the real thing when it comes along. You can also use the practice cast to give the line a slight stretch as this will aid casting, but don't overdo the stretching as it can damage the line. Once the practice cast is over I reel in until I have a sensible amount of line out that will enable me to easily cast 50 feet with no more than three false casts.

Boats

On calm days, or ones where there is only a gentle breeze, then fishing from the front of a skiff can be relatively effortless and the spare line will lie obediently on the front deck. By contrast, on a very windy day this is far from the case and the line will constantly be in danger of either being blown over the side of the boat or into the well and possibly catching on something. When fishing from a boat in very strong winds I always do a practice cast and then carefully strip back the line, loop it on the deck and then stand on it to prevent it blowing away.

It's worth pointing out here that whenever I am fishing from a skiff I never, ever wear shoes, so that I can always feel the line under my feet – this is important as there is nothing worse than unknowingly standing on line during a bonefish run with the inevitable consequences! My own personal preference is to wear thin socks as they stop my feet getting sunburnt, but I can still feel the line if I accidentally tread on it. If you are sharing a boat with another angler then they can play an active part in making sure the line is always where it should be; a good boat partner can be very helpful with line management when the angler at the front is making a cast on a windy day.

One of the great advantages of fishing whilst up front on a skiff is that it gives the angler a wonderful view of what's going on and it is generally easier, cloud cover permitting, to see bonefish much earlier than when wading. When the tides are running then the norm is to see groups of bonefish swimming towards you, so a cast that will put the fly at the front of the shoal and a fairly fast retrieve will normally do the trick. As the tide slows down and the depth of water becomes less, then the bonefish are likely to be encountered in ones or twos and a more accurate, challenging cast will be required. At times like this it is best to forget about the other people in the boat and just focus on the job at hand but, of course, this is easier said than done!

Because the boat angler is higher up than when wading the flat it is important not to have a belly in the line between the rod tip and the surface of the water when striping back the fly. If there is a belly, then the strip strike will not be so effective as it will have to take up the slack before making any contact with a bonefish. I always make sure that the rod tip is just an inch or two above the surface and pointing at the bonefish when retrieving the fly. This means that when a bonefish takes the fly, the line is as straight as it can be to the fish which usually gives a sound hook up.

Once a bonefish is hooked it is best to play the fish from the front of the boat, but when there are two anglers sharing the skiff the other angler should pull off some line from their own rod just in case more bonefish arrive on the scene, which is often the case. When this happens the angler playing the fish can step down into the well of the boat or to the stern. This gives the other angler a chance to get on the casting deck and start fishing – at times like this it is common to get a double hook up which can be very entertaining, especially when two big bonefish have been hooked at the same time!

The last important aspect of fishing from a boat concerns guides. The first point is that the guide should take into account your own wishes about what sort of day you want. Guides will not mind if say you would like to fish a certain area or you want to go lure fishing for an hour or so after lunch – they are there to make sure you have a good day and generally will do their utmost to achieve this. The other thing about guides is that poling a skiff is very hard work and especially so on very windy days, so I always insist that I stop fishing around lunchtime. This is to make sure the guide gets a well-earned rest. These breaks should not be considered to be wasting time, as they give everyone on the boat a chance to take stock of the morning's fishing, check leaders and flies and discuss tactics for the afternoon.

Over the years I have been very fortunate to fish with some really excellent guides who have been admirable anglers in their own right and my progress as a bonefisher owes a lot to them. Many of them have been more than willing to share their knowledge and experience. It hasn't always been plain sailing though, as in my early days as a bonefisher I did have some bad guiding experiences. However, this only served to highlight the good guides and I quickly built up in my own mind the attributes and qualities of a first-class guide. In summary, the really good guides enjoy what they do;

they are professional, knowledgeable and take genuine pleasure in seeing you catch fish.

Bonefishing from a skiff is quite different than when wading, but can be, in its own way, just as intimate and this is especially so when fishing for large, single fish that are cruising the shoreline. The one big advantage that fishing from a skiff has over wading is the view it gives the angler. On those clear sunny days, when every ripple, shadow and glistening bonefish tail is clearly seen, it can be a totally absorbing experience.

Acknowledgements

Thanks to Alan Gooch for his excellent design work and guidance on book publishing.

To Pam Stagg for her editing skills and attention to detail.

Roger Bailey for his photographic expertise.

David Tipping and Douglas Barnes for their advice.

A bonefishing trip wouldn't be the same on your own and I would like to thank the following people for making so many bonefishing trips memorable.

Firstly thanks to Trevor Ashton for being such a good boat partner and someone to discuss theories and tactics with over the years. Mention must also go to Phil Glossop, Chris Barnett, David Keens, Gordon Sutherland, Vincent Piriou, Pierre Perdrix, Jack Aley, John Gale, Bruce Sittler, Ron Courtoreille and Rob Roblesky for many happy bonefishing memories.

Another group that needs recognition are the special guides I have learnt from along the way. They are Docky Smith, Patrick Roberts, Rupert Leadon, David Neymour, Duniesky Urbano Otrega, Phillip Rolle, Elias Griffin and Manuel Chac. Thanks also to Betsy Sandstrom-Rolle for her excellent Thanksgiving dinners!

Finally, a very special mention to my wife, Sue who has shared some of my bonefishing experiences and encouraged me to write this book.